The Young Warriors

Arise, Shout, Pursue

The Young Warriors

Arise, Shout, Pursue

Wesley E. Smith

Treasure House
An Imprint of
Destiny Image® **Publishers, Inc.**
P.O. Box 310
Shippensburg, PA 17257-0310

"For where your treasure is,
there will your heart be also." Matthew 6:21

ISBN 1-56043-296-9

For Worldwide Distribution
Printed in the U.S.A.

This book and all other Destiny Image, Revival Press and Treasure House books are available at Christian bookstores and distributors worldwide.

For a U.S. bookstore nearest you, call **1-800-722-6774**.
For more information on foreign distributors,
call **717-532-3040**.
Or reach us on the Internet: **http://www.reapernet.com**

To Young Warriors Everywhere

Contents

Foreword

I first heard of Wesley Smith while serving as camp administrator at a church camp in Upstate New York. His name surfaced from time to time in conversations regarding past happenings at the camp. All I really knew about him was that he had been the speaker at a youth gathering at the camp, and that "strange" things had occurred during that weekend. Being somewhat curious, I invited him back to Beaver Camp for our annual Spiritual Life weekend. He graciously accepted, and my life was forever changed as a result! Nearly 15 years later Wes remains one of my mentors and a dear friend.

In 1985, the Holy Spirit used Wesley to introduce my wife and me to China with the words, "You can go!" As a result of that exposure, our family moved to Hong Kong in 1990 and we have been working in China ever since. Many other people's lives also have been forever changed by traveling with Wesley to China, Haiti, Africa, the Philippines, and other countries. Wes has always said, "I want to go where the fish are biting!" and the Holy Spirit has used him to send many workers to the mission fields. With an emphasis on the fact that age does not disqualify anyone from becoming one of the "Young Warriors," his teaching and preaching have equipped and enabled many, regardless of age, to run with the vision of David.

Fifteen years later I find Wesley just as intriguing as when we first met. I have rejoiced and cried with him through joys, victories, pain, and suffering. But I can honestly say that the trait I first found most attractive in him is just as evident today as it was then: Wesley truly enjoys living the Christian life! The Christian life is not a burden to him. He does not need to live up to man's expectations of him, for Wes answers only to the Lord Jesus!

In a nation where political correctness is the current fad, and in the church community where "religious correctness" is becoming all too common, it is challenging and refreshing to know that "religiously incorrect" individuals like Wes have not all been driven from today's church scene. While he may not be at the "big happenings" advertised in much of the Christian media, he will be found wherever there is a sincere and honest desire to touch the heart of Jesus!

If you are bound by religion and all of the things that you "have to do" to please Jesus and other Christians around you, this book may upset you. But if you are concerned that the joy of serving Jesus has vanished and that the victorious Christian life is extremely difficult to live in today's world, join with Wesley in casting all your cares on the King and enrolling in the ranks of the "Young Warriors," allowing the Lord to truly set you free!

Milo Kauffman, Jr.
Hong Kong, May 1997

One final note: I'd recommend reading and studying the Book of First Samuel to help you gain a better understanding of this book.

Introduction

*O*ur planet now has over five billion inhabitants. In China alone there are 1.3 billion human beings—with 42,000 newborns being added every day. Each of these people has a soul that will live somewhere for eternity. And each one of them needs to hear the gospel in order to be saved. Also, there are many signs that we are living in the last days (see Acts 2:17-19), and although it is not the purpose of this book to study eschatology, there is not much time left. If we are ever going to serve Him, then this is the hour.

God is raising up Young Warriors all over the world during this end-time harvest to fulfill the great commission. They are coming forth from every country, culture, and language group. These are the "Special Forces" in God's army at the end of the age. He is calling them in a way that is beyond human language to describe. And because it is the mind of God at work, it is beyond human capacity to comprehend. The living

God of the universe is speaking personally to individuals and placing a profound call upon their lives, and "Young Warriors" are those who hear from God and obey.

God is the Lord of the harvest and He is directing who goes where—and when. Young Warriors are messengers from God who speak the truth and are guided by the Holy Spirit to bring in this last, great harvest of souls to God's Kingdom. They are needed because the Lord has chosen to use people to spread His message. Jesus made it very clear when He said, "The harvest truly is great but the laborers are few, therefore pray the Lord of the harvest to send out laborers" (Lk. 10:2; see also Mt. 9:37-38).

God selects Young Warriors by their availability, not by their talent, good looks, or brain power. The Lord is looking for people, men or women, who will be available to Him and who have a heart after God. Anyone who sincerely opens his heart to God has the potential of becoming a Young Warrior and of being used by Him during this exciting era. Without a doubt, He will use you if you want to serve Him. He will anoint you with the Holy Spirit and with the power to serve Him. He doesn't need you to be anything other than available. *His presence makes up for any lack that we may have in our lives.*

Chapter One

Changes

So many people today are operating in the flesh; and all that they can produce is flesh. Flesh cannot produce spirit (see Jn. 3:6). For that reason, many leaders struggle and work very hard, only to see people betray them and their ministry become smaller and weaker. *How frustrating it must be to sink an entire lifetime of effort into a ministry, and at the end realize that you have merely shouted into the wind. Nothing is left and very little has been accomplished—for eternity.* Young Warriors desire to do better than this!

Young Warriors are called to be iconoclasts like the prophet Jeremiah. (An iconoclast is someone who attacks and destroys cherished ideas.) Jeremiah was told by the Lord to "uproot and tear down, to destroy and overthrow, to build and to plant" (Jer. 1:10 NIV). He could not begin building and planting until he had first uprooted, torn down, destroyed, and overthrown. The Young Warriors' purpose, like Jeremiah's, is not to destroy so that there is nothing. *The goal is to build and plant, but we must start with a solid foundation or the entire building will collapse!*

With 50 American churches permanently closing their doors each week, it is obvious that the building is collapsing before our very eyes. In modern America we have zero church growth. We have developed almost as many traditions as the Pharisees had in their days. They knew the Scriptures backward and forward, even setting large portions of them to memory. Yet, interestingly enough, when their Messiah, the Anointed One, actually showed up in person, they did not know who He was.

They did not know who He was! Think about the implications of this. If they did not know in their day—despite their amazing knowledge of the Scriptures—do you suppose that it might be possible for us, 2,000 years later, to be just a hair off center?

Many things in Christianity today are done out of habit, and are not based on the foundation of The Book. When questions are asked or suggestions are made on how things are done in church, the stereotypical responses are: "We've always done it this way." "As long as I'm in charge here, this is the way we will do things." (Forget about whether the "things" work or not. And, hey, all along we were under the impression that the Church belonged to God and that He was in charge!)

In some places the shortest route to the parking lot is via the wide avenue of question-asking or suggestion-making. However, I believe that every church or organization should have a suggestion box, and the suggestions should be read by someone, not just automatically trashed.

Why do we insist upon using Saul's armor instead of being like David and casting it aside? (See First Samuel 17:38-39.) Why do we think that just because something has worked for others or has worked for us in the past, that it automatically works now?

In the business world corporate owners try to find out what works and what doesn't work. *A wise business-man changes or discards anything that is losing money for the company.* This is how progress is made.

For example, the United States totally dominated the automobile market for over half a century. When the Japanese began producing small cars, many people made fun of "those pregnant skateboards." These little cars sold for about $2,000, and anyone who purchased one was almost humiliated by teasing from the owners of the huge, eight-cylinder gas guzzlers.

Then the oil crisis came along. All of a sudden tens of thousands of Americans wanted one of those little cars. Guess what? They could only get them from the Japanese.

The rest is history. Everyone in America now knows the names Lexus, Toyota, and Honda. I don't even have to tell you what kind of a vehicle I drive!

The Japanese not only produced a vehicle that was gas-efficient, but they also began producing quality vehicles that we in America didn't even know existed. Their cars were actually problem-free, instead of malfunctioning two weeks after purchase. Even the United Auto Workers' Union saw the handwriting on the walls. Suddenly, this union was demanding that the workers begin taking their work seriously.

The American people got a taste for quality and decided that they would settle for nothing less. They got a taste of the Japanese products, and the taste was so good in their mouths that they did not want anything else. The American automobile industry was in big trouble and they knew it.

At first they thought that they could smother the Japanese market by lobbying Washington against these "dangerous" Japanese imports. When that didn't work, they tried high-tech advertising techniques that bombarded the American people with the message, "Our cars are built better and are of superior quality."

But the American people were not as dumb as the manufacturers and slick advertisers had supposed. *Just saying that something is good quality does not make it good quality.* The car companies could advertise their tails off. Nothing would change. The people were hooked on a product that they knew was superior to what was being produced in Michigan.

The multimillion-dollar media blitz was a total flop, except for a few dupes who continued buying junk cars and then pasted bumper stickers on the back that read,

"I'm an American and I buy American." Well, guess what? I'm an American, too, and I buy Japanese. It's not anti-American to think for yourself and act independently. Proof of it is that the Japanese share of the United States' automobile market has now grown to 24.6 percent! *This is what the real America is all about—people who think for themselves.* The freedom to think and act has made our nation the most powerful country on the face of the earth.

So, guess what finally happened? Yes, dawn finally arrived and the big Detroit moguls decided that *they* would have to change—not the American people. When the purchasing public could no longer be manipulated, suppressed, or tricked (Note: that same idea is used in the Bible when discussing the "smothering" or "quenching" of the Holy Spirit [1 Thess. 5:19]), change was imminent.

The manufacturers began putting pressure on the employees to actually work and produce something good, something competitive. By the 1990's some of the American car companies had begun to catch up. But some choose to stay "blind" to what has happened. They still have not realized that if they don't produce a good quality vehicle, then the American people won't buy it.

Isn't the same truth relevant in the Church? If we close our eyes to the fact that what we are doing doesn't work, and that it hasn't worked for a very long, long time, then we are going to be left behind. God is for what works, and the Young Warriors whom He is raising up feel the same way. *Anything that keeps us from total victory must be trashed!*

Many Christians in America are very concerned about the fact that Islam is growing so rapidly. (There they go, buying those foreign cars again.) Would it ever dawn upon a congregation that maybe, just maybe, *we* need to produce something just a little bit better? Maybe we need to produce something like what is being produced in many countries overseas. Maybe we need to produce something like the Church in the Book of Acts produced!

Having the willingness to change is important. Fortunately, many of the automobile makers in the United States became aware of the fact that they actually have to make good, reliable vehicles. Because of this, American people again feel confident buying cars and trucks from some American companies and know that the vehicles will be reliable. If this were not so, then the Japanese would be dominating *more* than one-fourth of the market.

But what produced these changes? What gave industrial leaders the will to make changes? And on the spiritual scene, what will cause the Church to make changes?

The obvious answer in the automobile industry is that someone came along with a better product. The buyers sampled the product and liked it. They knew it was better than what they *had* been purchasing and using, and then refused to settle for anything less. Thus, American companies were forced to "shape up, or ship out."

Spiritually, we need to experience the same thing. Someone, or some group, needs to come along and show the Church that we can do better. We don't need a new product. There is absolutely nothing wrong with the Bible or with the Lord Jesus Christ. We simply need to return to the Bible in practical ways so that our joy will be made known to everyone. If you are happy, everyone knows it. If you are miserable, everyone knows that, too.

Too often we have displayed misery and, not surprisingly, we haven't had very many takers. I have actually heard individuals say, "I already have enough problems of my own; I don't need to join up with you church people."

Inside the Church we can protest as much as we want about this attitude. But until we display in practical ways that Jesus Christ truly makes our lives joyful, all of our words will be just so much hot air. We will be like the auto makers during their advertising blitz; no one will believe us. If the same sins dominate the Church that dominate the rest of society, then what message do we have?

In other words, until Christianity really works among us and lifts people up out of their misery, we have nothing to say or offer. We must ask God for the same power that was in the early Church and for the same power that we see being poured out in places like Toronto, Pensacola, Houston, and across the world. We are living during the greatest revival in the history of mankind, and Christianity is really the fastest growing religion in the world. These facts should make us so hungry that we will persist in prayer until we get what we need from our mighty God.

We certainly give credit to American companies who have changed and grown in response to the changing needs of modern consumers. And, in like manner, we give credit to American churches who have changed and grown in response to the needs in the lives of modern Americans. There is change in the air. There is a growing awareness that we cannot continue with the "same old, same old."

Seeing what is happening in other countries should make a profound impact upon us, too. It may take a little humility to admit that we are in desperate need of a revival that changes lives. Yes, it is a humbling thing to have to learn from the very people whom we have looked down upon. How could those "foreigners," those "savages," possibly do something better than we Americans? *How proud we have been to think that we have a corner on the God-market.*

For example, what an eye-opener it is for the first-time traveler to Europe to find that the highways there are consistently quality smooth. The highways are so superior to ours that there are no speed limits in rural areas. And there are very few accidents. (It is not easy to get a driver's license in Europe, either. Europeans who want a license must pass a very rigid series of tests, and also pay several thousand dollars.) It is not unusual for vehicles to travel 150 miles per hour! The first question that popped into my mind when I went there the first time was: "Why can't we have highways like this in the United States?"

Maybe another question that should pop into our minds is: *"Why can't we have the Holy Spirit moving in our churches like they do in other countries?"*

Could it possibly be (like the automobile industry) that we are going to have to get rid of some old attitudes and adopt some new ones? Could it possibly be that what we have been doing does not work well? And could we possibly make changes? Is it possible that we even care?

Because they do not change, Therefore they do not fear God (Psalm 55:19b).

Or are we in such a comfortable rut that we will merely close our eyes? *Going to church and rushing home to watch television is not what Christianity is really about.* If this is all that Christ's death and suffering on the cross means, then surely God made a very big mistake by sacrificing His only begotten Son!

The name of the game for the Young Warrior is staying alive and becoming a Life-giver. Sometimes that will require us to break the rules and ignore those traditions that have become religious "laws" over the years. Take King David for example.

Some people have criticized David's actions from the safety of their Sunday School classrooms. Yet, what an unfair thing to do! David wasn't attempting to form doctrine on a Sunday morning for the entertainment of the bored. He was fighting for his life!

Corrie ten Boom had no qualms about lying to the Gestapo in order to save the lives of Jewish people. And we have made a modern hero out of her. How much more so for David. He lied to the priest to get bread and weapons, acted like a madman, let his spittle fall down upon his beard, marked the doors of the city, and repeatedly lied and deceived Saul, Achish, and the Philistine princes. But this did not make him a liar or a madman. It's just what he had to do. He went for what worked.

How could he do these things and still be a man after God's own heart? Because in war time there are no rules. He was trying to stay alive. This did not make David a liar or a madman in the sight of God. God knew that he had to do these things in order to evade Saul and stay alive—and to keep the ragtag gang of his alive, too.

Frances Edward Smedley (1818-1864) once said, "All is fair in love and war!" The end-time move of God and the battle with satan is both love and war—at the same time.

At this late hour *one of our main goals as believers should be to stay alive—spiritually alive.* Death is stalking us at every turn, even in the Church. Five out of ten marriages end in divorce. Three out of every five girls in the United States have been sexually molested. Homosexuals have promised to stalk our sons and seduce them. AIDS, the first politically protected disease, is even killing the innocent among us. Television, presenting us with about 200 different channel selections, in many respects is an insult to our minds and our morals.

Politicians, who once demanded respect from the citizenry, are now thought of as dishonest and immoral. And some of the most famous movie stars, singers, and athletes are no longer wholesome role models for our nation's youth. Even the economists are bewildered about the future, and they contradict one another as they attempt to give good advice about a safe haven for investments. In urban areas decent citizens live behind lock and key, while the criminals roam free. And educators are bewildered as they see high school graduates receiving diplomas without being able to read. Truly there is a crisis in our society.

Almost everything in this world system and our society is attempting to strangle us and put to death the life within us. We may not be hiding in caves in Israel, but we are running for our lives. If this isn't the time for change, then when will it be time?

Young Warriors must plan to stay alive. (I have made a personal covenant with God to stay alive and keep as many people alive as possible especially my family). We must do whatever the Spirit of God guides us to do during this end-time struggle of life and death. *Our focus should be to stay alive—and to be Life-givers!*

If we don't stay alive, then we will not have life to give to others. One of the most absurd excuses I have ever heard for not praying in tongues goes something like this: "The Bible says that praying in the spirit edifies the person who does it (see 1 Cor. 14:4). I don't want to be selfish. I want to do things for others, not myself."

I can respond to this very simply: "If you are not built up (edified), then what do you possibly have to offer someone else? *We have to **have** something in order to offer something.*"

Would you be willing to apply that same logic to your Bible reading? your church attendance? prayer?

And if we have nothing to give to people except dead doctrine and rules, then, truly, we have nothing to offer them. Jesus came that we might have life and that we might have it more abundantly (see Jn. 10:10). From my observations, it would appear that the majority of Christians do not even have as much life as the world has. And that is very sad. It is a travesty, and Young Warriors intend to do something about it. *Young Warriors plan to bring Life wherever they go.*

Everyone may not want what we are offering, but there are always the few ragtag remnants who are so hungry for the real thing, that when it is offered, it will be received. (God has promised me personally that in every meeting where I speak He will put His hook in someone.) And *there **are** people who are hungry.* Some people are starving to death and don't even know it. They seldom take time out from their dull routine to even think about it. Others know they are starving and when they are offered good food, they gobble it up. They dig in and eat it.

If someone is thirsty, you don't have to beg him to drink. You don't have to "sing the invitational hymn for the fifth time." If food or water is available, that person will eat it or drink it. Have you ever been very hungry and then you sat up to the table? Do you remember how wonderful the meal tasted? No one had to force-feed you. *The end-time remnant person is the one who looks for life, and when he finds it, he enters in with great joy.*

So the Young Warrior saves his life, saves himself from this "perverse generation" (see Acts 2:40). He does it in many ways: herding sheep, throwing rocks at trees, carrying picnic baskets, slaying giants, playing music, or writing—whatever it takes! He has discovered that life is not found by making sure that all of the doctrines are lined up perfectly. *Real life is found by doing what his Father guides him to do, day by day,* not by following the dictates of man.

The Young Warrior's main concern is not making sure that he has a preprinted doctrinal statement to give to people, stating his doctrinal position. But neither is he ignorant of his rich heritage in the Church. He has read over and prayed over historical doctrines and finds nothing in them that contradicts his life as a Young Warrior. The opposite is true: Christian history reinforces what he believes and who he is. His main concern is with what works—what really works—and what brings life.

I have been asked on numerous occasions, "What is your doctrinal position?"

I consistently answer, "Read your Bible and you'll know what I believe. Also, I am for what works. Anything else is a sham."

However, for the benefit of those rare folks who like to read doctrinal statements, here are three that I have studied, prayed over, fully endorse, and believe to be true:

1. A Brief Statement of Faith
   Presbyterian Church (U.S.A.)
   (1983) (pp. 161-164)

2. The Nicene Creed
   (A.D. 381) (pp. 165-166)

3. The Apostles' Creed
   (8th Century) (p. 166)

If you are attending a church where people are getting saved and there is joy and gladness all around, if you see your fellow believers being creative and getting excited about how the Lord is leading them—then don't change anything. This message of change is not for you. But if you know that something is drastically wrong, and you want to do something about it—no matter what—then *deep has called unto deep in your life. You must respond.* (See Psalm 42:7.)

If you have come to a place in your spiritual journey where you know that true Christianity has to be more than what you are experiencing today, then you have received the call to become a Young Warrior. Answer the call!

The Young Warrior doesn't want change for the sake of change. The Young Warrior only wants change if there is death in the pot (see 2 Kings 4:40). So if your church is a soul-winning station and the people are happy and healthy, then don't change anything at all. More power to you. We are for what works here—not change for the sake of change. And if what you are doing is getting good results, by all means don't change anything. *Just praise the Lord, stay alive, and keep trucking until Jesus returns!*

Chapter Two

Letting Go

*B*efore I wrote this book, I did something that I had wanted to do for many years. I went up into the mountains where we have a small cottage and I spent three months reading, studying, praying, and hiking mountain roads. This made a tremendous impact upon my life. For over 30 years I have traveled extensively and, at times, I have been a very busy man. But lurking in the back of my thoughts was the feeling that I needed to spend a long time alone with God. I had faithfully read the Bible most of my adult life, but I knew that I needed to set aside a time to do nothing but listen to His voice and become better acquainted with Him.

One of the main reasons that I waited so long to do this was because I felt that I just couldn't spare the time. In other words, I could not bring myself to "let go" of everything for a few months. I felt that I was so important that if I faded off the scene for such a long time, then everything in my ministry would fall apart. How wrong I was! Things have never gone better since I "let loose" and disappeared for three months. Part of the result of those three months is the book you are now reading.

For those three months I spent several hours a day studying the Book of First Samuel. During that time some significant changes occurred in my personal life. It became very obvious to me that, like Saul, there were a number of things in my life that I was desperately clinging to. God had given all of them to me, on loan, of course; but as time had gone by, I began to think of them as mine. How easy it is to cross that invisible line!

God's gift of a ministry somehow becomes "my ministry." God's reputation becomes "my reputation." God's gift of a business or job somehow becomes "my business, my job." God's gift of a spouse somehow becomes "my spouse." His children become "my children." His Church becomes "my church." His home becomes "my home." His stuff becomes "my stuff," etc.

I've often heard Christians flippantly say, "Let go and let God!" My dear friend, that is easier said than done, believe me. These "things" can end up becoming so entwined within our souls that it takes a tremendous tearing from within to release them back to God—where they belong. *But the good news is that God can do it.* He does have the power to break us down so completely that we release it all back to Him.

Not an easy process! Pain. Pain. Tears. Begging. Pleading. Confusion. More pain. Over and over again, until we cry out from the depths, "Will this never end?"

This is not a "how-to-do-it" book to tell anyone how to release back to God that which is rightfully His. I've experienced it, but I still cannot tell anyone how to do it. All I know is that one day something happened inside of me and I suddenly found myself saying, "I don't care anymore. I just don't care. My entire life is yours, God—my entire reputation, my future, my marriage, my children—everything."

Strange. I had said those words before—years ago. But now I was saying them again. Only this time He had reached so far down inside of me that I meant it, *really* meant it.

I had not been unhappy like that in a long, long time—even before I was saved. Suddenly I had more joy than I had ever had in my entire life. But nothing had changed! All of the problems were still there. I could still see the sadness in my daughters' eyes from the death of their mother and from the horrible way that she died from ovarian cancer. I still faced many very complicated decisions connected with my new marriage. And "my ministry" was undergoing major changes. It was like I had been sitting on top of an erupting volcano.

But now none of those things weighed me down. I was free. If the volcano blew, then it was God's problem, not mine. I even gave Him my very painful, messed-up back, which I've had for most of my life. I heard myself saying to Him one day, "It's Your back. If You want it to hurt, that's Your business, not mine." And it made me laugh so hard. Suddenly I found myself laughing about the things that had tormented me so much and had even given me insomnia. Only those who have wrestled with those "night demons" know the horror and torment of not being able to sleep at night. And we all know that "good little Christians" are supposed to sleep like babies, especially those of us "in the ministry."

And I think that I even gave Him the volcano. "Have fun with it," I told Him. "If you want to blow it, then blow it. Let it erupt. But, remember, I'm yours." And I felt like I was!

I believe that I moved from being in Saul's shoes to being in David's shoes; so I know from personal experience that it can happen. God can reach into a Saul's heart right in the middle of his journey downward and lift him up.

For the rest of my life I will praise Him for what He has done for me during this study of First Samuel. What a hypocrite I was. When I started the study, I automatically identified with David and even bragged inwardly to myself, "I'm a David. I'm a Young Warrior. Look what I have done."

But God's Word is a mirror and it shows us who we are, not what we have done (see Ps. 119:9,11). *I quit looking at what I had done and began looking at who I was. It made me very ashamed.*

God's Word also washes us thoroughly (see Jn. 15:3), and I have been washed. I hope that I am a little meeker than I was before and that I have been humbled. I know that I have been set free. And I know that I am happy again and ready for His next adventure. I guess that is part of what being a Young Warrior is all about.

My five daughters and their husbands are definitely Young Warriors. They have all been overseas many times on "capers" for God—two of them live in Jerusalem! They know and have experienced the power of God. How grateful I am for who they are in Him. No father could be more thankful and proud of what Jesus has done, and is doing, with them and through them.

My oldest daughter, Lisa Bartow, wrote a few pages about letting go. Her personal observations on the first chapter of First Samuel are so appropriate and fit in so well here that I am inserting her quote:

"Picture Hannah. She's in church praying with all of her heart (see 1 Sam. 1:9-11). She's asking for something that she wants more than anything else...a son. She is desperate for a touch from God. She's so earnest before God that even the preacher thinks she's drunk or crazy! She is well aware of the fact that she and her husband cannot produce a child. Hannah needs a miracle...a miracle from the Almighty God.

"There's something about real honesty before God that moves Him. When my mom was dying of cancer, I needed a touch from God, too. I prayed like Hannah prayed…with tears, with honesty, with brokenness, with heart, with blubbering foolishness. I prayed a prayer that would make religious people cringe. I remember my words: 'Oh God, I can handle it if You take my mom, as long as I know that You're waiting for her…that You are out there. But God, if You don't exist, You can't have her! I need to know that You're really there!'

"A religious person would have given me a speech on the value of faith alone, or told me that my doctrines were wrong, or told me that all I needed was the Bible. I could have prayed a 'religiously correct' prayer, since I know how to do that. And Hannah could have prayed for strength to endure her barrenness, too. I knew that the prayer itself was 'crazy,' but God understands the heart.

"In a few days my husband and I met a big, bearded, leather-clad man in a restaurant. He was gobbling a juicy steak and sipping a cold beer. His beautiful Harley Davidson was parked on the sidewalk outside. For some reason we started having a conversation and soon he had pulled his enormous self up to our table.

"He began to tell us about his near-death experience of seeing Jesus. He told us that he became a believer as a result of that experience and that he had just returned from Central America as a missionary.

"If this same guy had been on T.V. in a slick suit with a big hairdo, I would never have believed him. God hand-picked this man because He knew me, He heard me, and He answered me! I don't remember the man's name who told me his story. But I do remember that it was faith in a living God that carried me through my mother's illness. I put my head down on the restaurant table and sobbed with relief. *God was waiting for my mom!*

"God met Hannah at the point of her honesty and need, too. It shouldn't be surprising that Hannah had a baby boy. What is surprising, though, is what Hannah did with that baby. After Hannah got her son, her heart's desire, her answer, she went against any mother's natural human tendency. She gave him away. What?! She gave him away! Not grudgingly...not with bitterness in her heart...not with sadness. She gave her son back to God!

"You see, Hannah was so grateful for what God had given her, so full of joy and adoration for what God had done for her, that *she willingly gave him back to God for keeps.* I think that if I had been Hannah, I might have tucked that baby under my arm and made Jonah look like a slowpoke in my haste to run away from God. I would have kept my precious gift to myself. But Hannah was different. She completely understood that Samuel was never hers to begin with! He was birthed by a supernatural God and belonged to Him.

"As we watched our mother die of cancer (before two of my sisters were even out of high school), our stabilizer was the same as Hannah's. My mom was God's gift to us from the beginning! She belonged—and does belong—to God. We had the privilege of giving her back. In any circumstances, an attitude like Hannah's can bring joy, peace, and fulfillment to your life.

"I have a life because God gave life to me. I have a car and a home because they were presents from an awesome Dad, my God. My kids are really God's, too. The church I attend was God's idea at the beginning—so was yours. Your salvation was God's doing. Your ministry was God's touch on your life. If this is really true, why do we hang on to our gifts with both hands and cling to them so tightly. *My* car, *my* ministry, *my* church, *my* mom! I guess *we really don't fully grasp what will happen if we give our stuff to God to use as He wants.* Not only that, but *we don't comprehend what will happen if we give ourselves to be used by the God who owns us!*

"My mother and father had five daughters, I being the firstborn. I can remember sleeping on a cold cement floor in the Philippines during one of our crusades when I was a young girl. I can remember eating spoiled seafood and trusting God for my life. I can remember riding for hours in a cattle truck in Haiti on the edges of 300 foot cliffs for Christmas. *My parents knew the secret that Hannah knew. They knew that their children belonged to God.*

"I would not trade my childhood for anyone's! I have reaped the fruit of having been given to God and then giving my own life and family to God. I have known, and seen, and experienced the awesome life-changing power of Jesus Christ and would never, ever, trade it for status quo Christianity! I wouldn't trade it for a white picket fence and a dog named Spot! I wouldn't trade it for mediocrity and the safety-seeking comfortable lifestyle that accompanies it.

"Hannah's kid ended up being used by God as one of the most famous prophets in the history of the world. He anointed the first king of the nation of Israel. He also anointed the second king of Israel, David, the king through whom would come the ultimate King, the King of the Universe, the Messiah and Savior of the world, Jesus Christ!

"I wonder if Hannah ever wishes she would have kept him to herself? I wonder if Samuel wishes he would not have spent his life in service to God?

"So what about you? Are you 'crazy' enough to ask God to do a supernatural work in your life? Are you painfully aware that without His intervention you are totally helpless? Are you willing to pursue God to the point of looking like a fool to the outside world, and even to organized religion? If you are, then look out...God is watching, listening, and answering! But that's only the beginning...

"This book does not approach First Samuel from a doctrinal angle. Instead, we should take off our religious spectacles. Hopefully, you, the reader, will see practical ways to apply the simple truth of the gospel as we trace the lives of two men, David and Saul. Much like Hannah, they had both been given a precious gift from God: kingship. The difference between their lives was how they handled what they had been given, and the choices that they made.

"You have also been given a precious gift from God. You have been anointed a king—a son of God—because of the redemptive power of Jesus Christ! How will you handle what you have been given? And what choices are you making? Are you holding on, grasping, groping, sweating, worrying, and almost making yourself sick—or are you experiencing the amazing joy of releasing everything back to Him?"

Samuel was really a miracle! (Maybe that is what every Young Warrior is: a miracle of God's creative power.) At the beginning he didn't even exist. In fact, it seemed that Hannah, his mother, could not even bear any children. In the Jewish culture being childless placed a stigma upon her and she cried out to God for an answer. She got so desperate that she told God she would give the son to Him if He would allow her to conceive.

When God answered her prayer, she was faced with a choice. Would she do what she had promised, or would she clutch the child to her breast and never let him go?

Considering what a mess the leaders of the Jewish religion were at that time, how could a mother who really loved her son turn him over to be raised by the likes of Eli the priest and his two sons, Hophni and Phineas? These two sons of Eli's were misusing the offerings that were being given by God's people. They were using the temple to do their own thing, and they made no qualms about it. They had sex with the women who came to worship. They didn't even try to hide what they were doing, and Eli just turned his head and closed his eyes to all of the evil that his sons were involved in. All of Israel knew what was going on and it made them despise the worship services (see 1 Sam. 2:12-15,22-25).

Could you imagine sending your young child into a place like that and letting people like that raise him? Yet Hannah sent Samuel into just that kind of atmosphere. She had promised God that she would give her son over to be raised in the house of the Lord, so she kept her promise and believed that God was bigger than the evil men who were in control of things. She totally released her son into the care of the living God.

Some would call this irresponsible! God looked at it as faith and He honored it. In spite of the conditions of Judaism at that time, God began to speak to young Samuel within the religious structure. A Young Warrior can hear from God wherever he is. Somehow Hannah knew this—believed this.

Some people use the excuse today that the church is so messed up, and so highly organized, and being run by such carnal men, that it is impossible to function as a true believer within its perimeters. So they have thrown the baby out with the bathwater.

Yet, Samuel's life proves these excuses to be wrong. And it shows what a praying mother can accomplish. Samuel was raised up to be a prophet of God and is one of the greatest examples of what a Young Warrior can be. He became a Nazarite, meaning "consecrated one." Like Samson, Samuel was dedicated to the Lord's service for life before birth. He was the last of the judges and the first of the classical prophets. His anointed life caused God to show His mighty power throughout the nation. God used him to bring major social and political transition at the end of the period of the judges: He anointed the first two kings of Israel, Saul and David.

Samuel operated out of his home in Ramah for most of his life. This is especially meaningful to me, since I have operated our entire ministry on a table in my home. Until this study, I had no idea that Samuel, too, had operated like this. Though he was never officially called a priest, he performed sacrifices and conducted worship at the shrine in Shiloh where the ark of the covenant was kept. We remember him for his extraordinary faith and his ability to intercede with the Lord. He became what God had promised: "I will raise up for Myself a faithful priest who shall do according to what is in My heart and in My mind" (1 Sam. 2:35). This is the very best definition of what and who a Young Warrior is—someone who will be faithful to God, and someone who will do what is in God's heart and mind! He is looking for such people today.

Although Samuel became even more than what his mother had ever dreamed for her son, his own children, Joel and Abijah, proved to be as corrupt as Eli's two sons had been. It was perhaps this weakness in Samuel's family that gave an opportunity for the elders of Israel to pressure Samuel to appoint a king and eliminate any future need for judges to rule Israel. "...Look, you are old and your sons do not walk in your ways. Now make us a king to judge us like all the nations" (1 Sam. 8:5).

Samuel was produced by prayer and kept by the power of God at a time when most people had lost respect for the house of God and for its leadership. God showed that through honest, sincere prayer, anything can be changed. This is the great challenge before us here in America. Young Warriors must believe that God is able to bring down that which is evil and replace it with what is in His mind and heart. But we must also take note of the fact that men often do not accept God's ways. After Samuel had been used mightily to bring respect back to the worship of God, the elders turned right around and wanted to organize it and do it their way. God's patience with His people is shown so clearly here. He allowed them do it their way, but, through Samuel, warned them of the consequences.

Little Hannah, with her big faith, not only produced a Samuel, but changed a nation.

Chapter Three

They Wanted a King

*Y*es, they did! The Israelites wanted a king, and they said so in no uncertain terms. They were tired of this "Invisible King" thing. They decided that they no longer wanted a theocracy (led by God); they wanted a monarchy (led by a king).

For about 300 years (1400-1100 B.C.) they had been led by judges. Before that, it was Joshua and Moses, the prophets. Now they had decided that they wanted to be like all the other nations around them. Nahash was the king of the Ammonites, Agag was the king of the Amalekites, Achish was the king of the Philistines, and then there were the kings of the Moabites, Edomites, and kings of Zobah.

Every nation surrounding them had a king, so it was only natural that they would want one, too. However, following our natural inclinations can lead us in the wrong direction. The Israelites overlooked one major reality. They already had a King who was taking better care of them than any earthly ruler, albeit He was invisible.

By wanting a king like all of the other nations (one that they could see), they were actually rejecting God, distrusting God. This was at the heart of it. And He spelled it out specifically for them: "But you have today rejected your God..." (1 Sam. 10:19). "...The Lord your God was your king" (1 Sam. 12:12).

So this was a very historic moment for the Jewish people. Inspired and born from a desire to be like everyone else, they were really changing their destiny and the way they would function as a people. Attempting to clutch and hold onto their national identity would inevitably cause them to lose it.

God has given each of us a free will. We can choose to believe in the invisible God and allow Him to rule our lives, or we can compare our lives to those around us and attempt to be like them. The choice is ours; and the Lord allows each of us to decide for ourselves. He wants to be our "King," but He will not force His rulership on anyone. His way is the way of the heart and the way of Life.

If it is not in your heart to have Him rule your life, then He will not insist upon it. And the consequences of your decisions will be yours—not His. So we really can't blame God for the way our lives turn out. We are the ones who make the choices. The time to consult Him is ahead of time, not afterwards.

He does have the power to open the heavens and scare the wits out of us. Then we would eagerly accept Him as King because we would be so incredibly afraid of Him that we really wouldn't have a choice. The day will come when every knee will bow and every tongue confess that He is God (see Rom. 14:11). But His real desire is to have a love relationship with us. He wants us to choose Him because we want Him. The Israelites decided to choose what they could see and they used the surrounding nations as their standard. The choice that they made more than 3,000 years ago continues to affect what is news-breaking in the Middle East today. How long-reaching are the consequences of our decisions!

This was a very tragic error in judgment. If they had only noticed—the other nations were terribly jealous of them! These nations were terrified by the fact that an invisible God was defending the Jewish nation. The destroying angels that God sent time and time again inflicted fear into the hearts of all of Israel's enemies like no earthly king was capable of doing. Repeatedly, and within just a few minutes, thousands of enemies were annihilated. Yes, the enemy nations were extremely jealous of the relationship that Israel had with this mighty and invisible God of the heavens!

How often we are blinded from seeing what we have and Who we got it from. The Israelites should not have looked to the world for their standard. Likewise, we do not have to glance in the world's direction in order to make major decisions. We don't even have to look to the religious world for direction. This was the Israelites' first mistake. Does it really matter what the world is doing? Does what they are doing actually have anything to do with us?

When I was raising my children, they would periodically remind me of the fact that "the other parents" let their children do certain things. I always replied, "What the other parents decide for their children has absolutely nothing to do with our household and how we make decisions in our home." How thankful they are now that I took that stand. And how thankful I am that I looked to God's Word for our standard and not to the cliche, "everyone's doing it." So what if everybody is doing it! As a child of God, that has nothing to do with you.

The Israelites made one of the worst decisions in their history by this trade-off. Imagine wanting to trade the living God for some carnal earthly king who would probably misuse them and treat them badly anyway. They had it made and they didn't even know it.

The nations who had their earthly kings did not have the King whom the Israelites had. But because the King of the Jews was invisible, the people had to walk by faith. They got tired of trusting in Someone they could not see, and therefore forfeited everything that they had. Little did they realize how jealous the other nations had been of them.

Throughout my 33 years of ministry, like the person in Robert Frost's poem, I have walked "the road less traveled by, and that has made all the difference." God called me from a teaching position to be available to Him—full time. That journey has taken me to places where I had never dreamed of going, both physically and spiritually.

I must admit that at times I have glanced aside to see what some of the other ministries were doing. And at times I have even been jealous. But each time that I was tempted to copycat someone and lose the creative flow of His Spirit, the Lord would speak ever so gently to me and remind me of my original calling. My main calling is to teach and preach the Bible.

For some believers this seems to be a very difficult way to go—this trusting in an invisible God. And so they, too, like the Israelites of old, have yearned for something tangible, something that they could see and touch, something, as it were, that they could sink their teeth into. Although this gives them some sense of security for a while, they end up missing the very Fountain of Life. What a sad trade-off!

Once you start down the road of trying to be like the nations around you, it becomes a trail with no end. Instead of being "the road less traveled by," it becomes the road, the wide road, that everyone is using. And we all know the final destination of that highway!

For those doing it the world's way, it becomes the great bondage of having a home in the right community, wearing the clothes with the popular labels on them, driving the smart vehicles, attending the proper schools, etc., etc. As we watch people struggling to make it financially today, it all goes back to this basic principle: Which king are you going to serve? Think how often the companies (and the "kings" who own these companies) laugh up their sleeves as they see millions of people purchasing their overpriced products, simply because they are the "in" items to own and show off.

And as is so often the case, the very people who want to look so different and unique, end up "in uniform," dressed exactly like the peer group they want to represent. In the malls it is so easy to categorize people just by the clothes that they flaunt. In their attempt to be so individualistic, they have completely lost their ability to be original—they all end up looking exactly alike.

It really doesn't cost much to live in today's society unless you are trapped into the kind of thinking that most of our fellow Americans are locked into. If you are willing to live a simple lifestyle and listen to the voice of your King, you will be free from what ensnares the rest of the people. On the few occasions that I visit the mall, the main thing I notice is how unhappy most of the people are. They walk the halls looking for one more material item to purchase, hoping that it will fulfill the vague emptiness inside their spirit. But shortly after buying yet another item, the post-purchase blues grip them and they find the same haunting loneliness emerging. And each time it gets worse. The "king" that they are serving cannot satisfy them.

Have you ever wondered why wealthy people commit suicide? They can buy anything they want, they can go anywhere on the planet, and they can do almost anything. And yet there is such an emptiness and lack of driving purpose in their lives that sometimes they end it all. In spite of observing this, most individuals still want to be in the place where they would have an unlimited amount of money to spend. And this blindness is passed from generation to generation. When will we learn that giving our offerings at the mall (the modern temple) does not bring inner peace?

I was able to raise five daughters and send them to college on a meager missionary income only because my King guided me and blessed me. One simple example: none of my girls ever had a cavity! That saved quite a bundle of money right there. We seldom visited doctors, either, although we do believe in them. We didn't visit them because we didn't need them. Our invisible King made us happy and took better care of us than any of the earthly business organizations care for their employees.

I have said this over and over again, "I still have not met any person whom I would like to trade places with or trade jobs with. I love what I am doing." Although Jesus is invisible, and it takes faith to follow Him, it is by far the superior way. Our ministry has no bills, has no payments, raises no funds, and yet has given hundreds of thousands of dollars away to missions. And all this without asking anyone for money!

It is easy to sleep at night when the invisible King rules your life. Many of the stresses that load most people down in our society today simply do not exist for those who choose the path of faith, of really trusting God. Having a king that you can see does not take any faith at all. To follow the invisible King takes a lot of faith—but it is that very faith that pleases Him. Without faith we cannot please God (see Heb. 11:6)!

So God told Samuel, "Let them have a king, if that's what they want! Give them a king and don't take it personally. They have not rejected you. They have rejected Me" (see 1 Sam. 8:7).

It is easy to feel personally rejected when someone we have tried to help decides to backslide. But this is not a personal rejection. That individual, from a free will of his own, has chosen another king. He has rejected the walk of faith. He wants to live by his senses, i.e., that which he can see, feel, touch.

For the rest of his life, Samuel faithfully taught the people. But in reality it was too late. They had substituted a king of their choice in place of the living God. *All of the best teaching in the world would do them no good until they came back and acknowledged their basic sin against Him,* repented of it, and asked Him to be their King again.

Like the Hebrew nation of old, many of us today have made the wrong choices, also. We want to have our cake and eat it, too. In real life this won't work, and it doesn't work in God's Kingdom either. It must be one or the other. We can't serve a heathen king and then expect God's blessings to be upon our lives. Well... if we do expect them, we will be sadly disappointed.

Like the Hebrew children, you are faced with a choice also. Is the invisible God (the Lord Jesus Christ) your King? Have you substituted another king in His place? Are you willing to come back to Him and allow Him to be the ruler of your life? The greatest freedom in the entire world is to have Jesus as your King!

When you make Him your choice, you will be so free, happy, and fulfilled that you won't need to worry about what the other people are doing. You will be free! You won't even worry about what other people are thinking or saying about you. Your main concern will be to please your King.

The Hebrew nation traded away the very Best because they lost their focus. Peter almost did it, too. He asked Jesus, "What about this man?" Jesus told him, "What is that to you? You follow Me" (see Jn. 21:21-22).

Pleasing Him is what brings us the kind of peace and joy that the world never finds. Deep inside, each one of us wants the real King. We can spend a lifetime walking down the broad road that leads to emptiness and a life without purpose; or we can use the free will that He has given to us to choose Him. The choice is ours!

Chapter Four

Saul: The Journey Down

*A*fter the Israelites insisted that a king reign over them, the Lord instructed Samuel to pour the anointing oil upon Saul's head. As he carried out these orders, he kissed Saul and said, "Is it not because the Lord has anointed you commander over His inheritance?" (1 Sam. 10:1b).

So Saul received the anointing and God gave him another heart. He was dramatically changed; but like all of us, for the rest of his life he had choices to make—choices that would determine whether his journey would lead up or down. Despite his many successes, Saul lapsed into a profound sense of failure and loss. Sadly, although Saul started off well, he ended up being murdered by a man from the very tribe he had been ordered to annihilate (see 2 Sam. 1:8-10).

Pride

The first thing that we notice about Saul is a humorous incident that takes place in First Samuel 10:22. He had already been privately anointed by Samuel with the holy oil, and had subsequently seen amazing supernatural events. Now all of the tribes of Israel had gathered for his public installation—the coronation. What an occasion! Thousands of people had assembled for this solemn and festive moment. Israel was about to have a king!

But, as the coronation was about to take place, Saul could not be found. Imagine the embarrassment of the moment. The entire nation was there in expectation of this major event, and the man who was to become their king was missing.

We do not know how long the ceremony was delayed, but it must have become a desperate moment because they actually called the priest and asked the Lord about it. It was the Lord who supernaturally revealed where Saul was hiding. "There he is, hidden among the equipment" (1 Sam. 10:22).

This would be a very funny story, were it not for the fact that this insecurity in Saul's life eventually caused him to be an utter failure as king of Israel. An inferiority complex often manifests itself as pride. Some of the people whom we think are so proud are simply hiding the fact that they feel very badly about themselves. A clear understanding of the cross of Christ is what each of us needs, for at the foot of the cross we are all equal. You are not better; you are not worse. You are equal.

Saul had hidden himself under the luggage. But, when they looked, there he was, just as the Lord had told them. Saul was head and shoulders above everyone else in height, and it must have been quite obvious to everybody that he was blushing from embarrassment. He was not only embarrassed about the fact that he had been hiding, but for those who had any discernment, he also must have sensed that his very soul had been exposed.

At this point we do not understand why Samuel did not discern Saul's problem and do something about it. We would expect that a man of his spiritual insight would have gone to Saul privately and said, "We need to do something about your deep feelings of inferiority before they ruin your life."

Yet before we are too hard on Samuel, let us realize that there have been many moments of discernment in our own lives where we have remained silent, too, until after the fact. And by then it is usually too late. How easy to step forward after someone's downfall and say, "I knew that this problem existed a long time ago, but I never said anything about it." Usually we don't want to risk being blacklisted by "the powers that be" by telling the truth. Perhaps we would do better to reveal some of this truth as the Lord makes it known to us. Many lives could be saved by some dear saint coming forward in holy boldness.

The Desire for Recognition

One would think that being selected by the Lord from among the thousands of men in Israel would have been enough for Saul. What an honor! What a privilege to be chosen by the Lord and called into His service!

But very often public ministry magnifies flaws in people's lives. This was certainly the case for Saul. Many people secretly suppress who they really are inside by never being in the spotlight. But once you are in the spotlight, everything shows—eventually.

Things began to show up in Saul's personality within the first two years of his reign. His son, Jonathan, was a valiant young man and listened carefully to the voice of the Holy Spirit. On several occasions God sent him out to do great exploits. He was always amazingly successful. The first time he went out he smote the garrison of the Philistines in Geba. Upon hearing the tidings of this achievement, Saul blew the trumpet and announced the victory throughout the land. The only trouble with this was that he didn't tell the whole truth. He did not give Jonathan the credit that was due to him. In fact, the message the people received was that Saul had smiten the garrison, not Jonathan. This was a blatant lie!

The kingship was a gift to Saul from the Lord. But we see him here already overlooking the fact that God had given him his place of authority. He apparently felt that he had to grasp it tightly or it would slip away from him. Will we ever learn that the same God who gives us our ministries, jobs, businesses, spouses, children, homes, etc., is willing and able to help us take care of them?

What is it in human nature that gives us the idea that anything is ours? Everything that we have and are comes from His Hand. We can't even make our hearts beat. *And the only way we can truly enjoy anything is by realizing that it is His—always—especially after He has given it to us.* We can only be free and happy when we keep this in perspective. This is true whether it is our ministry, job, spouse, children, finances, health, etc. Clutching and grasping to hold on always ends up bringing torment. I cannot tell you how many parents have sat before me with tears streaming down their cheeks because they can't let go of a child—and that child was "on loan" from God anyway. Somewhere along the line the parents began to think of him as "their child."

How much pain we could eliminate from our lives if, like Hannah, we would give Him everything, and not take it back. We should be able to trust Him with everything—especially since it was His to begin with. We did not even have the power to breathe the breath of life into ourselves, or our loved ones.

The happiest people I know are those who truly understand that it is God's to give and it is God's to take away. He owns it all.

The Lord gave, and the Lord has taken away, Blessed be the name of the Lord (Job 1:21b).

If only we could say, with the apostle Paul, "I die daily!" (see 1 Cor. 15:31) How free we would be if we would die to it all!

I think that Jonathan walked with God in such a way that his father's lie didn't bother him at all. He was pleased to be serving the Lord, his earthly father, and his country. If his father wanted to take the credit for his victory, it was all right with him. And his heart was so pure that he probably didn't even understand the full implication of the downward path that his father was on.

The pure in heart often do not notice, or care, how they are being used for someone else's purpose or glory. Both David and Jonathan are types of those who work with, or under, someone who merely holds the office, but does not have the presence of God in his life. It can become very uncomfortable!

You may be sitting in the pew and be the "Saul" of your church. Your pastor might be a "David" who is being harassed by a committee of "Sauls." Your pastor could even be a "Saul" who is using the ministry for his own selfish and egotistical purposes. Each one of us needs to examine his own heart before the Lord.

I looked at First Samuel 13:3 and noticed that "Jonathan slew" and "Saul blew." What a vast difference! Those who are hearing from and obeying the Lord actually get the job done. The others are planning, planning, planning.

Excuses

Repentance (one of the basic doctrines of the Christian faith) is God's way of keeping us on the right road— that is, the road that leads up, not down. In private counseling sessions I have talked with many believers who are concerned about whether or not they have committed the unpardonable sin (see Mt. 12:32). I always tell them that if they are concerned about it, then it proves that they have not committed that sin. Losing concern for whether or not we have sinned is the real danger sign; being sensitive about personal sin is usually a good sign. However, if all we do is concentrate on how wicked we are, we don't make progress either.

Saul lost this concern somewhere during his kingship and never recovered it. He sinned greatly by offering the burnt offering before Samuel's arrival. He just couldn't wait for Samuel, so he went ahead and entered into an act of "worship" that was completely reserved for the priesthood. And he did it with the full knowledge that he had no business making this sacrifice. His pride was poking out its ugly head.

Samuel was furious, and told Saul that he had presumed to perform duties reserved only for the priests, and his actions were foolish. He also told him that his (Saul's) kingdom would not continue. He told him that the Lord was really looking for a leader whose heart was like God's heart (see 1 Sam. 13:13-14).

You would think that Saul would have knelt and prayed with Samuel and asked for forgiveness. You would think that he would have even wept and been broken as the prophet of God confronted him with his sin. (Compare this with David's reaction when Nathan confronted him with his sin with Bathsheba in Second Samuel 12:13-17.) But not so. Instead, we find Saul beginning to offer excuses for his behavior. Already we see that his heart was becoming hardened. After hearing what Samuel said, Saul now had reason to be looking over his shoulder in fear of the man who would replace him as king of Israel.

When the Lord confronts us with our sin, we cannot simply say, "Oh, well." We must at that very moment confess our sin and ask Jesus to forgive us. This is how we keep from being hardened through the deceitfulness of sin.

Poor Judgment

Once we blatantly disobey the Lord, our minds become clouded and we cannot make good decisions. I have had people come to me for the "quick cure." They think that a short prayer over them is what they need. Maybe they have been making bad decisions for 25 years. The cure is not a prayer from the latest speaker who hits town, but a complete turnabout. Often there is some hidden sin, maybe committed and buried for years, that needs to be dealt with.

On a day when feasting and celebrating was in order, Saul commanded a complete fast for the entire army. Jonathan did not know about Saul's foolish order because he was too busy obeying the orders of his heavenly Father. He had received the inspiration to take on the entire garrison of the Philistines with only himself and his armor bearer. He was so eager to obey the heavenly calling that he forgot to report in to his father. He simply went out and got the job done while his father was trying to figure out what to do.

The Lord honored Jonathan's obedience by working such a dramatic supernatural victory that Saul's scouts watched the Philistines run away. When they reported back to Saul, he still didn't know what to do.

Actually, the victory had already been won and all they needed to do was celebrate. But no! Saul would have none of that. "If anyone eats one bite today, he will be put to death," he declared (see 1 Sam. 14:24,44).

Not knowing about his father's orders, Jonathan found some honey and ate it to strengthen himself after routing the Philistines. When Saul found out about it, he declared that he would have Jonathan put to death.

How clouded can a person's thinking become? Here, the very one who heard from God and obeyed God, and the very one who brought victory in the camp, was going to be put to death—and it was Saul's own son. *For the sake of keeping "the letter of the law" he was willing to have his own son killed.* That is the worst kind of blindness.

Only the people saved Jonathan that day. They stood up to their leader and declared an emphatic, "No!" to him. "As the Lord lives, not one hair of his head shall fall to the ground, for he has wrought with God this day" (1 Sam. 14:45b).

How many good people have been kicked out of the church or placed on someone's blacklist simply because they have obeyed the Lord! Someone once said that if you feel that you have to get permission before you can do anything, then you are being manipulated. There should be such freedom in the body of Christ that we should not have to hesitate when the Spirit bids us to go (see Acts 11:12). There may even be some rare moments when we don't have time to clear it with a committee.

We should not allow good people to be slaughtered. When we see a leader or a committee consistently making poor decisions, we must be bold enough to stand up and declare, "This is enough. Stop it!"

Perhaps a better solution is to surround leaders with good faithful people to help them stay on the right track, supporting them with prayer and wise counsel. "But in the multitude of counselors there is safety" (Prov. 11:14b). A leader should seek the advice of several other people before a major decision is made. If Saul could be as blind and arrogant as he was, then it is possible for present-day leaders to fall into the same trap.

From that day forward Saul never had one day of personal peace. "Now there was fierce war with the Philistines all the days of Saul" (1 Sam. 14:52a). Likewise, it is possible for a believer to retain his official title, "Christian," but live his personal life as a tormented man.

Rebellion, Stubbornness, and Deceit

The Lord gave Saul a very clear mandate: "Now go and attack Amalek, and utterly destroy all that they have, and do not spare them" (1 Sam. 15:3a). So Saul went out and slaughtered the Amalekites, but kept Agag, their king, alive. He also kept the best of the sheep, oxen, and lambs. He began to find himself unable to obey even the clearest mandates from God. And he certainly found himself falling short of Samuel's expectations.

Samuel confronted Saul about this blatant disobedience, too. But once again Saul ducked and dodged and offered excuses. The way a person responds to personal confrontation gives a world of insight into his character. A meek, humble person will usually thank you for attempting to help him. An arrogant, rebellious person will always be quick to defend himself, and completely overlook the help you are offering. One tactic that a person like this uses is to divert the attention to you, and begin to accuse you of things in your own life. A person who is rebellious and stubborn is always unteachable. He thinks he knows it all.

Even after being confronted by the prophet, Saul insisted, "I have performed the commandment of the Lord!" (see 1 Sam. 15:13) At this point in his life he was completely blind and unteachable. Samuel knew this, but still gave him a strong lecture: "Rebellion is as the sin of witchcraft, and stubbornness is as iniquity and idolatry. Because you have rejected the word of the Lord, He also has rejected you from being king" (1 Sam. 15:23).

Saul continued to hold the office of king for many more years, but he was operating completely under his own power as a man. The Lord had left him and he became despondent to the brink of madness.

Again, one would think that if a person received a strong personal message from a prophet like Samuel, there would be weeping and prayer. Being told that he is involved in witchcraft, iniquity, and idolatry should bring any believer to his knees. Yet we have all seen arrogant stubbornness and pride among God's people. It always leads to their downfall.

I once told a pastor that the people in his congregation were starving to death—he was not feeding them the Bible. He would leave the Bible on the podium and strut proudly around the auditorium, somehow thinking that what he had to say was better than God's Word. He immediately became defensive and informed me that it was a subjective judgment on my part.

I was kind, but firm. "Please read the Bible to the people. That is what they need. If you must walk around the room when you speak, at least take the Bible with you and teach from it."

He looked at me with a haughty smirk on his face and completely overlooked the fact that I was trying to help him, not attack him. Today, at the young age of 41, he can no longer walk—and neither does he have a church.

"…The Lord has torn the kingdom of Israel from you today, and has given it to a neighbor of yours, who is better than you," Samuel told Saul (see 1 Sam.

15:28). It is a solemn moment of decision when we have the opportunity to change, and then let the moment pass us by because we are too proud to repent. The kingdom was "rent" from Saul. We are like children clutching a security blanket. It appears that when we hold too tightly, it gets torn away from us.

The Evil Spirit From God
(1 Samuel 16:14-16,23; 19:9)

Saul had now reached a place on his downward path where he had crossed that fine line of no return. Don't even ask me where that place is! All I know is that we see this in Saul's life, and I have also seen it in the lives of some of God's people in our generation. The love and admiration Saul once had for David alternated with blinding fear, jealousy, and hatred of David's spectacular successes. Saul could not escape the constant, haunting, and tormenting thoughts that came to him with every mention of David. *David was a living reminder of where he knew that he should be with God.* But he had lost it forever.

Yes. *Our stubbornness, rebellion, and pride consistently chosen over God's way of operating brings us to a very dangerous place.* In Genesis 6:1-4 we find God unleashing evil spirits upon mankind because of his persistent bent toward wickedness. He sent serpents to bite, poison, and kill His own people (see Num. 21:6).

There are those who have a real problem accepting the fact that a loving God would send an evil spirit to torment Saul. I think that is why the Bible specifically mentions it five times. "An evil spirit from God was upon Saul" (1 Sam. 16:23 KJV).

David's music would soothe Saul's tormented mind temporarily, and he loved to have David come and play for him. The Bible says that when David played, "Then Saul would become refreshed and well, and the distressing spirit would depart from him" (1 Sam. 16:23b). But this was always a temporary deliverance. The root problems in Saul's life were not dealt with in a biblical manner.

So often we see people candy-coating serious problems—placing Band-Aids, as it were, on cancer victims—while looking the other way in the hopes that things will get better. Sickness like this, sin sickness, always gets worse with time. It never gets better. Ignoring the problem never makes it go away.

Samuel had spelled out some of the sin in Saul's life. But Saul paid virtually no attention to what Samuel had said to him. It seems as though sinning meant nothing at all to Saul. After all, he was the king. He was special. The rules were for everyone else. He was exempt.

Pride gives us the feeling of being a king, someone on top, someone above everyone else. Pride in its "nth degree" even causes us to place ourselves above God and what He says.

So no matter how much torment came into Saul's mind, he would not repent. He would ask for David to play his "sweet music," but that was all. He would only listen to what he wanted to hear.

Once I was counseling a woman and she told me how tormented she had been all of her adult life. Then she proceeded to tell me what would cure her. According to her, if I would pray the exact words that she dictated to me, then she would find deliverance. I told her that if she really knew how to deliver herself, then she certainly did not need me. *I also told her that I would not speak to God words that she had placed in my mouth.* She stormed out of my presence in anger and I have never heard from her again.

Some people really like the attention they can receive in counseling sessions, and they feast on being in the limelight of it all. They have no intention of getting right with God and getting to the bottom of their sin problem. They would rather be tormented than to change their lifestyle. I can't imagine getting to such a confused place in life, but many people almost glory in their anguish. They really have no intention of being delivered. They have made choices on their journey down.

"An evil spirit from God!" This almost sounds like a contradiction until we examine the serious consequences of rebellion, stubbornness, and pride. If God cannot help someone who is unteachable, how can you expect to do it? In actuality, a person like this cannot be helped. In our modern society it is not politically correct (or religiously correct) to think that someone is beyond hope.

Satan loves to use people like Saul to consume time and sap energy from God's people. I love to help people and pray with people. The greatest thrill for any Christian is to lead someone to the Lord and see the person get set free. But if I get the smallest whiff that the person is not serious and is only playing games—if I think that he is getting some sick gratification from the attention— then I will stop counseling that individual.

The hard fact of reality from the real world is that there are some people who will not get better. As God's people we need to discern between the honest seeker and the dishonest faker. Many a pastor has spent endless hours working with someone who was sent to him by the enemy, just for the purpose of wearing him down, wasting his time, and bringing discouragement. It makes a minister feel very much like he is a failure if he can't help someone who has serious problems. I have counseled pastors who have completely burned out simply because they have fallen prey to the "Sauls" who have come to them.

The Bible says that fear involves torment (see 1 Jn. 4:18). The Bible also says that ...God has not given us a spirit of fear, but of power and of love and of a sound mind (see 2 Tim. 1:7). Saul's fear of becoming king, continuing as king, and losing his kingship literally destroyed him. The evil spirit from God brought intense torment into his life. On several occasions Saul tried to kill David. He even tried to kill his own son with a javelin.

When Saul realized that David had a pure heart and had no bad intentions toward him, he promised not to seek David's death. But then he turned right around and tried to kill him again. At times he even broke down and wept. Crying is not always a sign of someone's sincerity. Saul was an emotional wreck. This broken-promise and attempted-murder cycle showed the confusion in Saul's heart.

A person like this is in such a confused emotional state that it is impossible for him to keep his word. He means well, but he cannot control the "demon" from within. The powerful force pulling him down becomes too much for him to resist. And the more often he yields to the downward pull, the less power he has to resist when the next onslaught comes.

A pattern of anger, jealousy, fear, and lying, are always clear indications of something gone awry inside a person's life. I'm not so concerned about a one-time sin in someone's life as I am concerned about obvious patterns. If there are patterns of good works, as the Bible says (see Tit. 2:7), then there are also patterns of wickedness.

When I am counseling someone who manifests certain behavior patterns consistently, then I know that some kind of sin is at the root of his troubles. The sure way to victory for this person is a clear, honest confession of his sins—and repentance! And, yes, deliverance from demonic influence is sometimes needed.

Dabbling in the Occult

When Samuel anointed David and the Spirit came upon David, "The Spirit of the Lord departed from

Saul" (see 1 Sam. 16:14). This left such an emptiness in Saul's life that it literally drove him insane. He became consumed by such exaggerated fear that his paranoia eventually became obvious to everyone.

Once someone has known the deep things of God, nothing else can bring fulfillment. God had departed from Saul, and in spite of the fact that he was king, wealthy and powerful, his inner spirit life was empty—without purpose, and extremely lonely. I have visited with people who once knew the tremendous joy of God's anointing and miracles. I know of nothing more heartbreaking than to look into the eyes of a person like this who has lost it all. Truly, that person is like a walking zombie, a walking dead man.

Saul was at this point in his life when he consulted the witch of En-dor. He was so desperate to have a touch of the supernatural in his life that he was even willing to defile himself by indulging in necromancy, attempting to contact the dead. This was not something that he did innocently. All Israel knew that it was forbidden by God to participate in such things. Saul had begun by disobeying in little ways. Now he was "main-lining."

And the person who turns to mediums and familiar spirits, to prostitute himself with them, I will set my face against that person, and cut him off from his people (Leviticus 20:6).

Attempting to contact the spirit world is equal to spiritual adultery in God's eyes. God feels the same way about this whoredom as you would if your spouse committed adultery. *This is serious stuff! It is impossible to bypass Jesus Christ and contact the spirit world without getting in serious trouble.* Some people use the excuse, "Well, I didn't know any better." Try using that excuse on a police officer the next time you get pulled over for speeding—and good luck!

As Samuel spoke to Saul through the witch, he said, "It is because of your disobedience that you are in this present condition. Tomorrow you and your sons will be with me!" (see 1 Sam. 28:18-19)

Upon hearing this, Saul's fear completely overwhelmed him and he fell down upon the earth, almost losing consciousness. (He was slain in the spirit, but it was the wrong spirit.) All his strength left him. He knew that the end was near.

For someone who had started out so good, this is a pitiful ending. He had the potential of having one of the most glorious lives of any person who has ever lived upon the earth. He could have been the king of Israel whose glory would have been spoken of throughout eternity. But, instead, his life is a shameful memory. The "clutching, grasping, holding onto, worrying, and thinking it is mine" syndrome caused him to lose it all.

The very next day, just as Samuel predicted, Saul and his sons were slain upon the battlefield. Saul had attempted suicide. His sons were killed by the Philistines. But in a strange twist of events, an Amalekite was the one who granted Saul his request by thrusting him through with a sword. Saul had attempted suicide, but like so many other things he had tried in his life, he even failed in this.

Our choices take us on a journey through life. We can choose to release back to God everything that He gives us, and get to enjoy life—or we can choose to hang on in desperation, and end up being tormented. We decide, and no one else, in which direction this journey takes us.

Chapter Five

David and Goliath

*T*hen Samuel took a flask of oil and poured it on his [Saul's] head, and kissed him and said, "Is it not because the Lord has anointed you commander over His inheritance? (1 Samuel 10:1)*

This anointing never left Saul until the day he died. In Second Samuel, chapter one, a young Amalekite came to David and said, "I killed Saul for you" (thinking that he would be rewarded). And David said to him, "How was it that you were not afraid to put forth your hand to destroy the Lord's anointed?" (see 2 Sam. 1:14). David, through all of his relationship with Saul, still respected the anointing.

Here there are two anointings, exactly alike, on two different people—the one in the verse above that Saul received, and the one David received (see 1 Sam. 16:13). *The main difference between Saul and David is what each of them did after they were anointed.*

You might remember another anointing, the first anointing, that some of us have lived long enough to remember, which took place in the mid-sixties and early seventies. But that was a quarter of a century ago. That's a long time ago. I lived through that. I have wonderful memories of that outpouring of the Holy Spirit. I preached through that all over the United States and around the world.

It was great! That first anointing was wonderful, but the fruit of it has depended entirely on what each of us did *after* we were anointed. Now make sure that you understand clearly: There was absolutely nothing wrong with the anointing that we received 25 or 30 years ago. And there was absolutely nothing wrong with the anointing that Saul received, either. It was genuine. It was real. It came from God, and it was identical to the anointing David received. But the choices that we have made along the way, since then, have made the difference!

And the difference is as great as the difference between Saul's life and David's life. The second anointing in First Samuel 16:13 is when David received his anointing. The Bible says, "Then Samuel took the horn of oil and anointed him in the midst of his brothers, and the Spirit of the Lord came upon David from that day forward...."

So we have Saul with the anointing, and we have David with the anointing. To me, what happened to David is a type of a new anointing. Many people look back to a time when they received the Holy Spirit. I don't think that we should be looking back; we need to be looking to today and forward. Without the anointing we can only operate from the flesh, *but what is important is what we do after we have been anointed.*

Saul was anointed, but he kept making bad choices and his journey was always downward. He could have gotten up in church and said, "I remember when Samuel anointed me." But that would not have done him one bit of good if he consistently disobeyed the Lord. You can go to conference after conference and have great experiences (I call these people professional conference attenders), but when you come home, if you don't obey the Lord in your daily life, it was all for naught. You may have heard the greatest speakers in the country, but it won't do you any good unless you obey your heavenly Father.

The potential was there, and David always respected that in Saul's life, but Saul seldom tapped into the potential within him. That power had been placed there the moment Samuel anointed him and the Holy Spirit came upon him. In other words, Saul didn't do anything with what he had. And he knowingly chose to disobey God.

The first day that he received the anointing he saw more miracles than most people see in a lifetime. How exciting! This was meant to be a foretaste of what his entire life and ministry would become. But it never happened. He chose for it not to happen.

Even though we are anointed, we have a free will. The anointing will never leave us. "For the gifts and the calling of God are irrevocable" (Rom. 11:29). But we have the personal responsibility of choosing to obey the Lord each day.

Saul was anointed privately and David was anointed publicly. When Saul returned to his home, he was reluctant to tell his uncle what Samuel had done to him. Why are we so reluctant to share with our relatives? We love them the most, but we keep the Truth from them because of fear, embarrassment, or not wanting to offend them. This would be something like if Billy Graham anointed you and then you went home and wouldn't talk about it. Saul got off to a bad start right there in his own home and with his own people.

In First Samuel chapter 17 we find David is a little sheepherder. We know that it was God's intention to take him from the sheepcote to the throne. (The "sheepcote" is the place of beginnings; the "throne" is that place in God where He wants you to be.) So what do you do after you receive an anointing? David went right back to what he had been doing before. All of his relatives knew that Samuel had anointed him because they were there in the meeting and saw it happen. But David didn't think that he was above herding sheep.

One thing that has gone wrong with some people is that right after receiving the Holy Spirit, they immediately go out and try to do things in the flesh. After all, weren't they anointed? Someone has described them as "an accident looking for a place to happen." They never learned to relax. It is not our job to do something with the anointing. That is God's job. We don't have to do one blooming thing, except to be faithful where we are, and obey. In my own life I remained as a high school teacher for one full year after I had been anointed.

I think that one of the earmarks of the new anointing is that it makes you feel relaxed inside. So just relax. David did. He herded the sheep, protected them from bears and lions, threw rocks at trees, played music, and wrote poetry—and was happy doing it.

After all, it is God's program, not ours. We are not supposed to be struggling and trying to raise money for one thing after the other. Just relax. Wow! And it really works. We've relaxed and the result has been that we have been able to give about three million dollars away to Young Warriors who are going about their Father's business! Don't ever try to tell me that this doesn't work.

A joyful, free attitude of the heart will cause more things to be accomplished than all fleshly efforts combined! God will kill the devil off in two seconds whenever He feels like it. The anointing gives you such a peace in your inner-man that you are fulfilled doing the most simple things. So just go up there and herd a few sheep. Just sit around the wood-burning stove and be faithful in little things until your Father speaks to you to do something else. Let the Father initiate it.

That is what happened to David (see 1 Sam. 17:17). David's father spoke to him while he was there being faithful out in the field with the sheep. Isn't it strange that some people think that God is limited to speaking to us within the confines of the "building with the cross on top"? I've been some places where there was so much nonsense going on inside the building that it completely drowned out the voice of the Holy Spirit. And it is His voice that we need to hear.

Yes. God is able to speak to us wherever we are: in the car, in the shower, at work, at school, at play, mowing the lawn, and even in church. There is no limit to His ability to speak to His Young Warriors.

With your anointing you are guaranteed that the Father will speak to you—sooner or later. Discard all of your preconceived ideas as to what He is going to tell you. Be open! He is a God of surprises.

David's father asked him to carry a picnic basket of corn, bread, and cheese to his brothers who were out on the battlefield fighting with the Philistines. This was not a religious thing at all! No matter how religious you are, you can't make anything religious out of a picnic. Unbeknown to David, he was beginning his journey from the sheepcote to the throne. Sometimes great things emerge from insignificant actions. (Contrast this with Saul's journey from the throne to suicide.)

For who has despised the day of small things?
(Zechariah 4:10a)

David's father told him, "Take this picnic basket to your brothers and see how they are doing. And then come and tell me what has been happening to them out there in the valley of Elah."

Now remember, this was the beginning of his journey with the anointing. David was moving in the anointing, whether he knew it or not. Those following Saul were moving under leadership that was making bad choices, and they were not accomplishing anything at all. In fact, they were embarrassed, humiliated, and defeated—filled with fear, just like Saul.

Goliath had been coming out there for 40 days, twice a day, daring someone to fight with him. The Israelites were all terrified. Goliath came out there and humiliated them 80 times before David arrived with the picnic basket. That is a lot of humble pie to eat!

Now, little David came on the scene; and we see his obedience. The first thing he did was make sure that the sheep were taken care of. He found someone to watch them while he was gone. (Every step of the way we see the high character of this Young Warrior. No wonder he was "a man after God's own heart.") David didn't get so excited about carrying out his father's orders that he forgot to take care of practical matters. He found a keeper for the sheep, *then* he started getting excited about carrying out his father's new, expanded orders.

He didn't know it, but he had just graduated. He was being promoted. Sometimes you know it and sometimes you don't. The main thing is to be faithful in what the Father speaks to you.

David obeyed his father. Early the next morning he headed out toward the battlefront with the picnic basket. He thought he was on his way to a picnic, but he was really on a mission to deliver a nation!

When he arrived at the valley of Elah, he greeted his brothers and visited with them. About that time, Goliath, who was over nine feet tall, came out and defied the Israelite army.

As I was meditating upon this passage, I realized that in most communities we don't even know the name of the ruling principality, much less have the victory over him. The Israelites at least knew his name and were aware of who the enemy was. They were not spending their time fighting each other.

After David watched Goliath come out and humiliate the entire army, he began asking some embarrassing questions: "Why doesn't someone kill him? Why is he allowed to do this to God's people? Why should Goliath be allowed to defy the armies of the living God?"

Oh, that we would ask some questions like this today! Why have we allowed satan to humiliate us so? Why have we allowed him to devour an entire generation? Why are Christians as bound by sin as "non-Christians"?

As David began asking questions, it made his oldest brother, Eliab, very angry. At times, simple truth can hurt, can't it?

Sometimes the very people whom you would expect to be able to talk to—your brothers—are the very ones who turn on you vindictively. This is a normal defense tactic of the human psyche, and we see it manifested constantly in politics: When the heat is on, then accuse your opponent and divert the attention away from you.

Eliab scorned David and publicly rebuked him: "Why did you come down here? Who did you leave those few sheep with? I know that you are proud. I know how naughty your heart is. You only came out here so you could see the battle" (see 1 Sam. 17:28).

We know that all Eliab's accusations were false; David was completely innocent. The only reason he was there was because he was obeying his father. But do we find David defending himself? Absolutely not.

Sometimes the very people whom you think will get excited about bringing victory to the camp end up being your greatest critics. But why would your brother become angry simply because you want Life? Why would your brother be angry because you desire victorious living for everyone? Why would your brother be angry because you know that God has more for His people than what they are experiencing? One would think that a brother would want the very best for fellow believers—not the worst.

Perhaps the answer is found in the fact that your brother no longer believes that victory is possible—under any circumstances. Just as God's people could not hear Moses because their pain and suffering was so great, your brother may not be able to hear the message of hope because his life is so filled with pain (see Ex. 6:9). Therefore, he becomes convinced that there really is no hope. Your brother may go through all of the religious motions, but he really doesn't believe anymore. Your brother may have forgotten that God is able to save to the uttermost (see Heb. 7:25). He may be like the frog who was slowly boiled to death, and he now accepts the status quo as being real Christianity.

David now found himself on a much greater mission than that of delivering a picnic basket. (Isn't it great that he didn't get sidetracked into trying to raise money so that he could provide a picnic lunch for the entire army?) At this point he saw why he was there, and not even the wrath of his eldest brother—someone who should have understood—could dissuade him. *When the light dawns upon us and we discover why we are here, things begin to get very exciting.*

All that David offered in his own defense was, "What have I now done? Is there not a cause?" (1 Sam. 17:29). "Can't I even speak? Who is this uncircumcised Philistine that he should defy the army of the living God?" These are powerful rhetorical questions!

Why have we put up with this embarrassment for a quarter of a century? Why have we had to live with this death, this reproach?

David continued asking the questions until it came to the attention of King Saul. Even Saul, who needed a victory here in the worst way, tried to discourage David. "You are not able to fight with this Philistine. You are just a young person. Goliath has been a soldier for a long time. He has the training. You don't have any military experience."

It was then that David dipped into his memory bank and rehearsed to Saul how he had killed a wounded bear and a lion. I can just hear him saying, "The same feeling that came upon me when I killed the two of them is upon me now! I'll go kill him!"

David wasn't going out to have a wrestling match with Goliath. His intention was to kill him. Boy, does this cut through all of the religious red tape! David broke just about every doctrine in the demon manual. This gets right to the bottom of the thing, and says: "I'll take care of it right now. And it won't take my God long, either."

Whew! Don't you just love God? We don't have to continue allowing our children to become dope addicts, to get pregnant out of wedlock, to be homosexuals, etc. We don't have to crawl back into the church and be like everyone else. We don't have to sit by and watch another generation get ravaged. We can actually do something about it. Young Warriors plan to kill this thing dead. They are going to do something about it— either in or out of the church! Let's pray that a transformation will take place from within. There are so many wonderful people inside the structured church who are longing for someone with the anointing to come along and show them a better way—the way of Life!

At this point in the story a very comical thing took place. But it really shows how entrenched a person's thinking can become. Saul persuaded David to get dressed up in his armor, his helmet of brass, his coat of mail, and his sword. How interesting! Although this had not worked for Saul, he still wanted David to try it. Why did he think it would work for David? I guess it was because that was all that Saul knew. He didn't have any fresh, creative ideas. All he knew was the old wine and the old wineskin.

Why do we insist on using methods that have never worked? And why are we too stubborn to adapt to new ways of the Spirit?—especially in light of the fact that an entire generation has been lost?

Not only could David not fight Goliath while dressed in Saul's armor, but he also could not even walk! He didn't seem worried about offending Saul by not wearing it. He simply removed the armor and said, "I cannot walk with these; for I have not tested them" (see 1 Sam. 17:39).

David had to use what would work for him. And he knew what he was going to do. He was going to use his sling and a rock! It is what he had practiced with for many years. It was what he was used to. It was what he was comfortable with. And it just made good sense.

Using a sling wasn't anything new. Judges 20:16 says: "Among all this people were seven hundred men who were left-handed; every one could sling a stone at a hair's breadth and not miss." This was a common weapon, but no one in all of the Israelite army thought about using it. Or, if they did think about it, they were too afraid to try. There was only one vulnerable spot that Goliath had, and it was only about the size of a stone. If you missed, think of the consequences.

David did not think about missing. Many folks have concentrated so much on the fear factor that they have done nothing. Doing nothing is the surest way of losing the battle. How many battles have been lost because of fear?

Goliath attempted to intimidate David, like he had done to the rest of the Israelite army. He cursed him, disdained him, and tried to put fear into his heart. But David's purpose was set. He felt the anointing, the same feeling that he had had with the bear and the lion. So even though Eliab, Saul, and Goliath attempted to discourage him, David listened only to the inner voice of his Father.

Actually he not only spoke to Goliath, but he also prophesied to him:

But I come to you in the name of the Lord of hosts, the God of the armies of Israel, whom you have defied. This day the Lord will deliver you into my hand, and I will strike you and take your head from you. And this day I will give the carcasses of the camp of the Philistines to the birds of the air and the wild beasts of the earth, that all the earth may know that there is a God in Israel. Then all this assembly shall know that the Lord does not save with sword and spear; for the battle is the Lord's, and He will give you into our hands (1 Samuel 17:45b-47).

Oh, what we can learn from David's short speech! Regardless of where we go to church, and regardless of our doctrinal beliefs, can't we all agree that "all the earth needs to know that there is a God?" With all the troubles today, surely the world needs to know that there is a God like David's God.

This end-time anointing is for God's glory. It is to let the world know who God is and that He exists. The new anointing is not for puffing up some man's ministry. We've seen enough of that, and it has brought so much embarrassment to the body of Christ that some believers are even ashamed to call themselves Christians. And it is not because they are ashamed of Jesus. They are simply ashamed to be identified with what is being passed off today as Christianity. Would you have picked up this book if it had been named "The Christians"?

"The battle is the Lord's" is another statement that David made. Will we ever learn this? How often do God's people sweat, labor, and experience burnout, only to see things become worse. We are living in a time when 50 churches each week are permanently closing their doors in America. Perhaps it is time to ask some questions. Perhaps it is time to take off the old armor and adopt a new way of doing things. New wine must be put into new wineskins so that *both will be preserved.* Maybe we should actually try something that will work.

The battle between David and Goliath lasted less than 30 seconds! Think of it. Goliath had humiliated the entire army for 40 days. Then, one anointed young man was brave enough to ask some questions, and brave enough to go out and try. God did the rest!

I believe that the stone was guided by the Lord to Goliath's one vulnerable spot. Of course He used David's skill, too. And the battle was over just that quick. Then, to top things off, David stood over Goliath, took his sword from him, and cut off his head. *Both the Philistine and Israelite armies were spellbound as they saw David standing there with the huge head dripping blood.*

What a dramatic change in attitude! The entire Israelite army arose, shouted, and pursued the Philistines (see 1 Sam. 17:52). Up until then they had been filled with fear and they fled from Goliath every time that he presented himself. Why this sudden change in attitude?

One Young Warrior obeyed his Father! The rest is history.

This shows us how badly we need the anointing for this end-time ministry. We have some giants who need slaying, too. We need the anointing just as much as David needed it. Many wonderful things happened a quarter of a century ago. But the real sad thing, the heartbreaking thing, is that we have almost lost an entire generation to television, sex, and drugs.

Many people have looked back and said, "I was anointed. I was anointed." But they have overlooked the purpose of the anointing. God did not give it to us so that we could feel good, become professional conference attenders, and be puffed up with pride. He did not give it to us so that we could become an exclusive little spiritual club of Pharisees. He gave it to us so that we could make the same journey David made: from the sheepcote to the throne.

In the process of our mission, had we chosen to accept it, we might have changed an entire generation! But, instead, we have lost almost an entire generation. Many believers have watched their sons and their daughters being butchered by satan, and they felt that they could do nothing about it. They have watched helplessly as the devil has devoured their children, ravaged them, and destroyed them. The things that so many churches are proud of—expensive buildings, real estate, accoutrements, and degreed staff—are now haunting them in silent mockery. Many of these same people are now hanging their heads in shame because of what they see taking place inside the church: families breaking up, girls getting pregnant, kids getting hooked on drugs, sexual promiscuity among the clergy and laity, and even the fact that there is a debate in the church about homosexuality and bestiality. What's next? Will the church condone child molestation, serial killing, and cannibalism, too?

My God, how desperately we need the new Young Warriors to emerge who will do something with the anointing they receive. How can we still be bragging about the anointing we received long ago and the multi-million-dollar churches we have erected when, right before our eyes, we have lost the most precious commodity that our country produces—*our children*?

Instead, we should be weeping for the children who have been sacrificed on the altar of materialism, love of money, and greed. This is why we need an anointing!

Saul and David are obviously types of leaders today. Saul is like a leader of a ministry who holds the office and title, but he doesn't have the move of the Holy Spirit in his personal life. David is the man who doesn't necessarily have the title and the degree, but the Holy Spirit is moving powerfully in his life.

As I was studying this, I thought, *Now that is very interesting*. Then the Lord showed me something much deeper. Saul represents an entire generation that has been lost! Every hour in America 300 homes are broken into, 75 people are robbed, 12 are raped, and 3 are murdered. *Every hour!* And that does not even account for the hundreds of innocent babies who are butchered—sacrificed on the abortion altars of sex worship. Shedding the blood of innocent babies will never atone for the sins of fornication and adultery. "If we just murder the baby, then no one will know that we are whoremongers."

Abortion clinics not only need to be permanently closed, but there also must come a national repentance of the sexual sins that have spawned and supported the abortion merchants. This sinful behavior is what pays the fat salaries of doctors who are butchering babies. Closing the clinics is not getting to the root of the problem any more than closing the breweries got to the drinking problem during prohibition. In fact, during prohibition people drank more.

Ministers must thunder once again against sin—and spell it out specifically. People need to know that they will spend eternity in hell for participating in fornication and adultery. We need to stop worrying about whether or not we will offend the rich people singing in the choir. The truth must be told. The modern Young Warrior is no more afraid to tell the truth than David was to hurl the stone. The stone slew the giant. Truth will heal the land.

David represents the generation, the remnant, if you will, that God is raising up during these last days. There is a remnant of Young Warriors who are coming forth in power during this endtime. This "David" group is a ragtag church, led by the Holy Spirit! And we need to get excited about it because we are going to see giants slain by this ragtag gang. Already the Young Warriors are emerging.

Recently Gunther and Martha Fussle spoke at our church. They are from Zurich, Switzerland, and they are about the most precious couple that you could meet anywhere—humble, sweet, radiant, joyful, and together, really together. They stood on the platform holding hands and talking, without notes. They spoke from their hearts, back and forth, first one, and then the other. Just that was powerful in itself.

If you know anything about Switzerland and its beauty, you also know how reserved the people are. I have been to their wonderful country several times and have had the joy, among other things, of climbing to the summit of the Jungfrau. The view from that mountain peak is spectacular. So what this couple told us was especially amazing to me.

They said that they got together with eight other couples and decided that they were really fed up with religion and all of the trappings that accompany it. Together they made a covenant that they would not be a "church," but that they would simply be available to the Lord. They were hungering for real Life and they knew that what was being peddled to them as Christianity was a total mess, based completely on this world's system of money and power.

They had already been through the whole charismatic thing, and they knew that God had so very much more for His people. *Just going through the motions of being religious was not satisfying them.* They wanted what they knew the Lord had for His people, and they desperately wanted to be used by Him.

They started in their home on their knees with open Bibles—and no agenda! Today their home cannot contain the 2,000 people who are gathered around them, so they meet in a horse corral.

This couple was very precious in their faith, and as they told us about what was taking place in Zurich, a great hunger was created in our hearts. Speaking English, but with a very strong German accent, they said, "We just decided that a few of us were going to be available to the Lord. We met together with no program and no agenda to see what the Lord would do with us."

How precious! Today they are the largest and most powerful body of believers in Switzerland. And it is scaring the wits out of some of the onlookers in the city. Many Christians are even jealous of what the Lord is doing with them. *The Fussles and their 2,000 friends have a new wineskin with new wine in it and the Christians don't even know what it is!* But they are the talk of the religious community.

Other churches are nervous about them, but Gunther and Martha keep reassuring them, "We are not a threat to you. We are not even a church. You have nothing to worry about. We are just available to the Lord." But church leaders worry anyway.

And, boy, did this couple drop a bomb in our church when they spoke to us. They told us that they had been going along in this way for about two years, when someone got the idea that they should have a Bible-reading marathon. So they thought, "What could be wrong with reading the Bible in church?" (Think of it: actually reading the Bible in church!)

God says something in Psalms 138:2b that is amazing: "For You have magnified Your word above all Your name." Think of the implications of this verse. If God magnifies His Word even above His name, then we should at least hold the Bible in equal respect.

They got the idea of a "Bible-reading marathon" from observing the fact that in most churches you are lucky to get a verse or two per week. The rest of the time the speaker drones on and on with his own little ideas that cannot, and do not, feed the inner spirit. Man's word is a very poor substitute for God's Word.

My son-in-law and daughter live in Jerusalem. They both read, write, and speak Hebrew. They told me the following fact: Even now Jewish Orthodox scribes show very great respect to the name of God. When a scribe is copying the Old Testament and he comes to the word "Yahweh," or "Lord" as we know it, he lays his pen down, gets up and washes his hands, and comes back to the desk to write His name.

If this much respect is given to the name of the Lord, and the Bible says that "He magnifies His Word above all His name," then we need to honor His Word, too.

So the Swiss group decided to read the Bible, non-stop, for four days, day and night, 24 hours a day. They took turns reading aloud for 15 minutes each. The only time anyone was allowed to enter or leave the corral was every hour on the hour. They told us that some people came with their sleeping bags and stayed the entire four days.

They said that at first it seemed a little silly to "just have someone reading the Bible out loud" over the public address system. But as the time continued, *it was like the God of the Old Testament descended upon that place and filled them with His Glory. A power built in their midst. He came and honored His Word!* People were saved, healed, delivered, and blessed beyond imagination. Families were reunited. Husbands and wives reconciled. Children rejoiced! Financial problems were resolved. *Impossible situations that some individuals had struggled with for years were instantly evaporated—vaporized!*

How simple! How profound! A sling and a rock. A Bible and a reader. Why have we insisted that worshiping the Lord be so expensive and complicated? We have committeed and organized ourselves to death! Why do we have to pay a man an $80,000 a year salary to read the Bible to us—and then that doesn't even happen? How much does it cost to open a Bible and read it aloud? Why does the Bible have to be read to us in multimillion-dollar buildings? How expensive, do you suppose, was David's sling and rock compared to Saul's armor? *As God's people, we need to be for what works and what gets the job done—not what looks slick, modern, and "in."*

When I heard the Fussles tell their story, I could scarcely restrain myself. I stood to my feet and challenged our congregation to have a Bible-reading marathon, too.

In busy America there is really very little time given to His Word, in or out of the church. By the time the announcements and time-wasters are over there just isn't time to squeeze in God's Word—well, maybe a few verses. What a rush we are always in! Hurrying to get where? But why do we always have time for what we want to do? *I wonder how God feels about consistently having last place in Christianity—about consistently being placed on the back burner.* I think that we know how He feels about it. The lack of power and joy in the church tell the whole story.

What a shame. Bible ways get Bible results. Man's ways get man's results. The Bible has been placed on the back burner for too long. Where did we ever get the idea that man's word was superior to God's Word? If we don't believe this, then why do we give so little time to actually reading the Bible in church? To assume that people are studying it on their own is a serious oversight. We seem to have plenty of time for our favorite television programs. We seem to have plenty of time to do what we want to do. We seem to have plenty of time for everything else. Why don't we make time for God's Word? And when will we ever learn? After we have lost another generation of children?

Did you know that the early Church read entire books of the Bible when they assembled together? When a letter arrived from Paul or Peter, the entire epistle was read aloud to the whole congregation—men, women, and children. That was why after sitting in church for 40 years they actually knew what was in the Book. Many Christians whom I meet today don't even know the basic facts of Christianity (see Heb. 6:1-2), much less the deep things of God.

Now the ragtag group in Switzerland has a man who teaches the Word to them. He is surrounded by these nine couples who pray for him and help guide him. They keep him straight and he feels secure. The people feel good, too. A good leader surrounds himself with strong, good people. A weak leader surrounds himself with "yes" men, and the end result is that they all end up in the ditch.

May we learn from our brothers and sisters in Zurich!

God *does* have an anointing for this end-time generation. Almost an entire generation has gone astray. Saul never lost the anointing. God does not take back that which He has freely given (see Rom. 11:29). Up until the day he died, this anointing remained with him, but he was just going through the motions of his kingship. We need to do more than look backwards to a brighter day. The new Young Warrior is always looking to the future and to the time when his Father speaks a new word of instruction.

One doesn't have to be very bright to realize that we don't want to be like Saul. We don't want to be stuck in that old way of operating. We want new wineskins for the new wine. But, unfortunately, Saul does reflect so very much what is taking place in the Church today.

Many of us have been in it and we wondered why there was no life there, why there was death there, why there was defeat there, why there was humiliation there—right words, right songs, right hands raised, but no life. Everything was doctrinally accurate and religiously correct—but no life.

And this is what you always want to ask yourself, "Is there life or death here?"

I can attend a new church and within five minutes tell if there is life or death in that place. The first thing I do is look at the young people. If they are all seated in the back rows (placing themselves as far as possible from our "religion"), that is a statement in itself. If they are sitting there staring at the floor or fooling around with each other, then I know that there is death in that place. I'm talking about the kind of death that was in Saul's life. He lived, but like a lot of people today, he was a walking dead man.

I get so excited when I speak at a church and all of the young people are seated up front, singing, praising, testifying, dancing, and shouting. I love to see young people on the worship team playing their instruments with joy unto the Lord. Some places where I go the young people almost take over the service with dancing and praise and joy. It is not difficult to know that there is life in a place like this.

And then I glance over at the pastor. He is aglow with his own joy from watching the Young Warriors in action, and he is so fulfilled. It shows all over him. He is thrilled to know that many of them will run past him. He knows that this is a credit to his own ministry, not a personal threat to him. Nothing pleases him more than to see some of his young people go out and accomplish great things in God's service.

I wonder how Billy Graham's pastor felt when he watched him become the greatest evangelist this world has ever known: And I wonder how a man feels when after a lifetime of ministry, he has not produced one Young Warrior!

We need to get hungry for this fresh anointing. Believe me, God has so much more. We just need to take the time to look for it and wait for it. And do we need it! It is not enough for me to look back to 1965 when I received the baptism of the Holy Spirit. That was a great experience and I will never forget it. But I have to live now and move forward into the twenty-first century. Looking back won't cut it. Looking back won't bring life to me or to others. I must obey God now, like David and Jonathan did. That is where the life is. And *the key to the whole thing is consistent study of the Scriptures—and obedience.* We must listen carefully for that small, still voice.

I need the same kind of anointing that David had so that I can go forth and do something with it. Saul could brag about his anointing, but he didn't do anything with it. And I think that's why we've lost almost an entire generation. We've played church. We've flown off to "how-to-do-it" conferences. We've had our little church services and tried to do the right thing. We have even criticized our children for the way they dress, not realizing that we were losing them to something much greater—drugs, sex, a life without purpose, and sometimes even suicide, simply because we were not giving them something to live for.

A lot of those charismatic church services had more death in them than the mainline denominations that we came out of. And that is really sad! *In some settings the only thing the young people have learned about God is that He is boring; and they have also learned how to become good liars.*

So it is either time for a new anointing or it is high time that we do something with the anointing that we have already received. There is a remnant left who are hungry for real Christianity, and they know that what is being peddled to them is a fake. There is a growing number of people who, like David, are beginning to ask some very embarrassing questions.

God bless the leaders who see the potential of new ideas from Young Warriors and implement them. We have entered a time now when church leadership is getting hungry for the real thing and is willing to make any changes that will bring God's presence.

A person with the anointing likes to think. He likes to improvise and be creative. He loves to watch God take the thoughts that He gives him and cause them to become reality. This is creative. This is life. This is fresh oil, fresh anointing. This is real living. This is fun. These are the ways the sons of the fresh oil operate.

The Young Warrior wants the purposes of God to come to pass more than anything else. He craves it; and he knows that all of God's people need His healing power. So many people in the church have the exact same problems as the "heathen" do outside the church. The divorce rate is the same. We have as many fornicators and adulterers. We have as many pedophiles. We have as many wife beaters. The list goes on and on. Don't these facts ring bells in anyone's head? Do light bulbs ever come on?

Many a pastor is run ragged just trying to "maintain" his people, just trying to keep them afloat. Forget about all those heathen out there who need to be saved. At this hour and in this generation we are so busy trying to get the Christians saved, that we haven't begun to think about anything else.

God wants us to think! David and Jonathan both thought creative thoughts that led them into great supernatural experiences. God greatly honored them as they attempted to carry out His plans. *God is open to any questions. There is nothing that we cannot ask Him.* He will never get mad at us. He will never kick us out. There is nothing too sacred to discuss with him. He wants us to tell Him all that is in our hearts. If pulpit prayers bore you, then think what they do to God. So pray from your guts, from your heart, from the secret places in your mind.

If most Christians ever heard me pray in private, they would think it was blasphemy. But God likes it. Blasphemy to Him are the "now I lay me down to sleep" prayers. That was great when we were little children, but now He wants us to do much more than repeat memorized prayers.

In a marriage you would be bored silly if your partner said the exact same things to you every day. You want to be able to discuss up-to-date things with your spouse. God feels the same way about us. *One of the greatest tricks and deceptions that satan has put forward is to make us think that God likes fake, long, flowery, religious prayers.* Somehow we have gotten the idea that this is the way we are "supposed" to pray.

That is why you will hear many people say, "I just can't pray in public." What they really mean is that they do not know how to put together flowery and nice-sounding prayers. But *anyone can talk honestly from his heart to God.*

Since God is so open to all of our questions, perhaps we should be open to the good, honest questions being put forward by today's youth. Like David, they might just ask the one question that will liberate all of us. Why shouldn't we be open to questions and new suggestions?

I believe that God's people should be open for new direction, open for correction, open, open, open. And *the creative power of God is just as available today as it was in David's time.* It is the same God and He has not changed. He will pour His creative thoughts and power down upon us.

He has promised that in the last days He will pour out His Spirit upon all flesh—especially upon the youth! (See Acts 2:17-18.) And this is what we want. This is what our inner man is craving. It is what we are hungry for, and it is the only thing that truly satisfies us. The stale manna of yesterday has putrefied. Nobody wants to eat it, especially the young people.

But Jesus Christ has come that we might have Life and have it more abundantly. What are we waiting for?

Chapter Six

David and Saul

David and Jonathan

*S*aul's son Jonathan and David became dedicated friends. They both recognized the anointing in each other's lives. In some strange way, perhaps because of the blood line, the anointing Saul had received seemed to affect Jonathan and was passed on to him. The relationship that David and Saul should have had was transferred to Jonathan.

Consider the power that Saul could have had during his reign as king if he would have known how to tap into David's talents and work in unity with him! As we will see, he looked upon David as a threat and spent most of his life trying to kill him—instead of fighting the real enemy.

Jonathan's wonderful friendship with David eventually placed him in a very difficult position. His father was king, but he knew that eventually David would replace him. In the meantime he had to walk the difficult tightrope of trying to keep peace between the two of them. It proved to be an impossible task.

Thousands vs. Ten Thousands

As David went out with the presence of God, he became a mighty warrior. Of course, he had become instantly popular throughout the nation just by killing Goliath. Unbeknown to David he had aroused the envy and jealousy of his superior. The Young Warrior was soon to enter into a warfare that would, at times, almost bewilder him.

Every generation has known the power of music. Music has a way of communicating beyond any other media. We don't know who wrote the song, but people began singing a song with the refrain in it, "Saul has slain his thousands, and David his ten thousands." Once a melody becomes popular, not even a king can control it. People were singing it everywhere.

Saul became furious. He interpreted this as public humiliation. *A bigger man would have been proud that a Young Warrior under his command had done so well.* Had he only known, he could have used David's popularity for his own benefit. But he was not a bigger man. He sulked and plotted.

The surrounding nations soon picked up the new refrain, too: "Saul has slain his thousands, but David his ten thousands!" The song became so popular that it was even repeated among the Philistines. Saul became so angry and jealous that from that day forward he "eyed" David. He knew that his days as king were numbered and that David would replace him.

Jealousy and Murder

The very next day the evil spirit from God came upon Saul and he prophesied in his home. David, faithfully doing the job he had been asked to do, played the anointed music. Suddenly, without warning, Saul hurled a javelin at David, attempting to pin him to the wall with it. Perhaps David's keen sense of discernment saved his life. He was able to move out of the way just in time to save his life. I believe that he knew something like this was inevitable.

Two different times Saul attempted to kill David like this. David would be playing, and then suddenly Saul would hurl the javelin. David was very brave to continue serving in such a dangerous capacity.

Saul became so infuriated and frustrated in his troubled state of mind that he even attempted to kill his son, Jonathan, too. But none of his attempts succeeded. Obviously, the Lord was protecting both of them from this madman.

Types

It doesn't take much insight to see the modern parallel to this relationship. There are some Christians today who have lost the presence of God in their lives due to disobedience. Some of these people are even ministers and priests. Then they begin to feel very threatened by anyone who really is in touch with God. A lot of it is a matter of pride.

How amazing that when Jesus' birth was announced, the revelation came to shepherds out in the field, not to the priests and government officials (see Lk. 2:8-20)! God often chooses to speak to the "little" people— those who may be despised by those higher up the social ladder. Some of the most humble, uneducated people have come to me over the years with words of wisdom so directly from God that they have changed my life and ministry. When we shut ourselves off from receiving from the "sheepherders," we may completely miss what the Lord is doing in our generation.

At first there was a love between Saul and David (see 1 Sam. 16:21).This is kind of like the honeymoon in a marriage. Later, when it's time to take out the garbage and do dishes, things can change. It didn't take very long for the real spirit in Saul to make itself known.

As people in the congregation continued to "sing the song," jealousy, envy, and even hatred begin to consume Saul. Finally, Saul was unable to conceal his true feelings of jealousy and anger any longer, and those around him began to notice his strange behavior. Left unchecked, eventually it destroyed him.

We have seen very prominent, popular television ministries go down the drain for this very same reason— disobedience. It always brings great sadness to the body of Christ and the ramifications are eternal.

God bless the leaders who can rejoice when those within their congregations become giant killers! God bless the leaders who praise God when they see those whom they have trained and discipled going forth to do greater works than they have done. God bless the leaders who are thankful for those raised up under them who begin to see and do things that they have never even thought of doing. God bless the leaders who can receive from those who are "lower on the totem pole" than they are. *God bless the leaders who know how to groom a David or a Jonathan and cause their congregation to become a powerful force for God!*

Truly these leaders will be blessed. And, actually, it will be to their credit. Even those in leadership can join in the song if their hearts are right with God. Really, there is no place for jealousy or pride in God's Kingdom! If we as leaders never produce anyone who runs past us, then we are the greatest of all failures. Some men never know what they have missed by not experiencing the joy of watching a Young Warrior fly past them.

At my age one of the greatest joys I have is hearing about the exploits of those whom I have taught. It thrills me every time I find out that one of these Young Warriors is where he is because of some seed that I sowed into his life. I've been in the ministry long enough now to have people come up to me and say, "Twenty years ago in a meeting where you were teaching the direction of my whole life was changed." This is like music to my ears. Nothing is more rewarding for me.

That's why I am always telling Young Warriors, "This thing gets better, not worse! The longer you serve God, the more you begin to see how rewarding it is. When you first begin, you don't have as much to inspire you. You don't fully realize how powerful and eternal the Word is that you are sowing into people's lives. But wait a few years! When Young Warriors begin coming to you and telling you how much you have helped them, then it will make all of the pain and labor worthwhile. If only one person's life was made better through your efforts, that would be reward enough."

If you have never had a javelin hurled at you, consider yourself blessed and protected. But *if you have been truly anointed by God, you will experience every one of David's trials during your lifetime.* It is inevitable. Expect it. The javelins will be hurled in your direction.

I had an amazing thing happen the very week I was writing this particular chapter: I had to dodge three javelins, the same number thrown at David. At least we have clear teaching from God's Word to alert us as to what is taking place. For David it was a learn-as-you-go ordeal. He had to learn by the seat of his pants, so to speak.

The only advice I have for you if you are in a David/Saul relationship, whether it be in your church, or on a job with someone over you, is *listen very carefully to the voice of the Holy Spirit.* I am often asked by people if they should leave their church or place of employment.

I can never answer this question. It is too personal in nature. But I do believe that if your spiritual life is threatened by being where you are, then you should consider moving on. David had enough common sense to leave Saul's palace after the third javelin episode.

As you read these pages, you will learn what to expect in the future. The David/Saul combination almost always deteriorates into a very ugly scenario. (On some rare occasions the "Saul" actually breaks down under the stress and gets his heart right with the Lord.) Actually, it is spiritual warfare. The spirit in the person who is jealous of you wants to destroy you. Always remember that the real enemy is not the person in the congregation, the pastor, your boss, or the committee. For we don't wrestle against flesh and blood (see Eph. 6:12).

You have two very powerful weapons that are much sharper than the javelins hurled in your direction—prayer and fasting. Gossip and backbiting are not part of your arsenal and they will not do you or your situation any good at all. They will have a very negative effect in your life. But prayer and fasting can break down the most impossible situations. Arguing with your "Saul" will only make things worse. Exchanging harsh words will only escalate the animosity between the two of you. Even attempts at reasoning probably won't work. Remember, the proud spirit in the man is jealous and angry, even hateful. It is beyond reason.

Watch David and attempt to model your life after his life. I cannot conceive of anyone conducting himself in a more superior manner than he did. He never retaliated or tried to hurt Saul. He merely kept himself alive. You, too, as a Young Warrior must stay alive at all costs. You are no good to God's Kingdom if you are spiritually dead.

Treachery

After offering David one of his daughters as a wife and then giving her to someone else, Saul then offered David his other daughter, Michal. He knew that this daughter had some of the same spirit in her that was in him, and that she would be a "snare" to David (see 1 Sam. 18:21). Hoping that David would get himself killed by attempting to deliver the dowry, Saul proposed that David kill 100 Philistines within a certain time frame. David went out and killed twice that many Philistines and brought their foreskins as proof of his accomplishments. There was nothing for Saul to do but to give Michal to David as his wife.

Now David was more than just a servant; he had become Saul's son-in-law. But from this point on Saul saw clearly that the Lord was with David and he became even more afraid of him. His fears began to dominate his life and thinking. He counted David as his enemy continually.

Like many people in the Church today, Saul was now focusing on someone who wasn't even his enemy. In reality David was not Saul's enemy. But in Saul's mind David became the enemy. *If ever the Church needed to be fighting with the real enemy, it is today. God forgive us for ever spending any time fighting with each other.*

A good friend of mine is a Marine Corps Drill Instructor. He told me that very often his men will begin fighting with each other when they do not have any opportunity to go out on real missions. How true this is in the Church. If God's people never have a chance to actually go out and do something exciting with their training, then they begin to turn inward and self-destruct.

Kill David

From this point onward Saul made no bones about it. He ordered Jonathan and his servants to kill David. Jonathan, whose allegiance was definitely to David, told him about it. So David was on the run.

Many of the Psalms reflect the experiences that David had during this period of his life. No wonder he pled with God from the depths of his being for protection from his enemies. How wonderful it would be if we could go through life without any enemies, especially enemies from within the family of God. But it is not to be. Jesus told us very clearly that if we serve Him, then we will suffer persecution. *All who live godly in Christ Jesus will experience the discomfort of this type of warfare.* It is part of the calling for those with the anointing. The apostle Paul was forewarned that God would show him great things he would suffer for the cause of Christ (see Acts 9:16). Our job is to make sure that we are not suffering because we are rascals, but suffering because we are truly obeying God, suffering for righteousness' sake.

It is not a pleasant thing to discover that someone whom you thought was your friend would like to see you dead. It hurts a lot, deep inside, to learn that a brother has spoken badly about you behind your back. These are some of the mild javelins that get hurled our way. Some of God's people have even been physically killed because of someone's wrath and jealousy. There is no limit to satan's wickedness. Don't be so naive as to think that it can't happen to you. Satan despises the presence of the Lord in your life more than anything else and he will do anything to take you out.

This does not mean that we should live our lives in fear. It really is an adventure, and a fun one at that, if you keep a biblical perspective. *It simply means that you are in the process of going from the sheepcote to the throne—that place in God where He wants you to be.* What a journey! And if you don't like the prospects of this journey, then consider the path that leads in the opposite direction—the one Saul took.

The Cave Adullam

When you serve the Lord, it always attracts people. And *the people who come to you are not necessarily the ones you would choose.* As David fled for his life, he found refuge and a temporary place of safety from Saul in a cave named Adullam (see 1 Sam. 22:1-6). (You can still visit that cave in Israel today.) By this time about 400 men had attached themselves to him, even though he was on the run. Some people are very attracted by adventure. Without a doubt, David was living a very adventurous life by this time.

Soldiers from Saul's army were constantly stalking him with orders to kill him on sight. David was nobody's dummy. He knew that one way Saul could get to him would be through his family. So he moved his parents to Moab for their protection. God gave him grace with the king of Moab, and the entire time that David was on the run, his family was in safe keeping. He had even told the Moabite king, "Please let my father and mother come here with you, till I know what God will do for me" (see 1 Sam. 22:3).

In the cave David was in a bewildered state of mind. Think of the enormous changes that he had to adjust to in such a short time. Because he was so young, he was able to make the adjustments. An older person would have had a very difficult time being uprooted like that. He had been living in a peaceful village with his parents and working for his father as a shepherd. Now he had no roof over his head and he did not even know what he was doing from day to day. His only solace and comfort was that he knew God was with him, and that He would guide him.

It would be many years before God would make things clear to David. And for about ten years he was tested almost beyond his ability to take it. Eventually, he even had to leave the cave with his ragtag group. He didn't have an air-conditioned auditorium in which to worship God. He worshiped God on the run and the Lord caused him to escape from every attempt on his life. At one point 3,000 of Saul's elite soldiers were sent out to find him (see 1 Sam. 24:2).

No wonder the Psalms are so powerful and have helped countless thousands of people over the centuries. These passages from David's pen came forth from his soul. At times he was praying for his very life. We should never overlook the great miracles that kept him alive during this time.

Yes, you can even get into trouble hiding in a cave. *The roots of your walk with God are in the spiritual realm. You can go to the most remote place and the devil will still be stirred up against you.* And, yes, the ragtag group will seek you out and want to hang out with you. Some people live such boring lives that they are willing to go almost anywhere for a little adventure and life.

How interesting that "...everyone who was in distress...and everyone who was discontented gathered to him. So he became captain over them..." (1 Sam. 22:2). He not only had the personal responsibility for his own life, but now the burden also became even greater: He became responsible for the lives of 400 men and their families, too. *Now, instead of herding sheep, he was caring for real people with real problems.* And I am sure that many of the people who came to him were not very desirable people. He probably would have been "ashamed by association."

God was using the cave of Adullam to purify David and make him an even greater man. What a shock it must have been to many of David's earlier companions when, years later, he actually became the king of Israel.

Try to think about the contents of letters you might write to your family and friends from Adullam. Would any of your acquaintances understand? Perhaps some of them would be there with you. Some others would never understand or empathize with you.

My own father watched my life for over five years before he believed and understood what God was doing with me. His prayers had raised up a Young Warrior and he didn't even know it. I told him, "Dad, I have become what you prayed for all of these years." How surprised and delighted he was that Jesus had answered his prayers! And what a joy it was for me to have my father's full emotional support during my years in the cave!

I will never forget the beautiful spirit I saw in my father on his death bed. His last prayer with mother and me, in spite of his intense pain, was a prayer of thanksgiving—a prayer of thanks for all that God had done through us and with us. He never asked for anything during his painful hours of dying—even up until his moment of death. But he did tell me something that had been very difficult for him to say before: "I love you!" He was 94 years old when he left this life.

Saul's Obsession

By this time David's ragtag army had grown to 600 men. Foraging as they went, and often traveling by foot and living in the wilderness, David began to whip them into a powerful fighting force. They were no longer just some slipshod, fly-by-night, vagrant group of people. Under David's anointed leadership he was shaping them up into a team that he could be proud of.

Instead of fighting with his real enemies, Saul was now spending his full time looking for David and chasing him through the mountains, woods, and rocky deserted places. The Bible says that "Saul sought him every day, but God did not deliver him into his hand" (1 Sam. 23:14b). *How much time has been wasted by God's people as they have wrestled with each other, and as they have been in power struggles with each other over trivia—majoring in minors—while the children of this generation go into a Christless eternity!*

Saul's Robe

Saul and his "Special Forces" came to the very cave where David and his men were hiding. So David's ragtag team hid in the sides of the cave. Saul decided to enter the cave and relieve himself.

David's men urged him to kill Saul, and even told him that the Lord had provided the opportunity for him to do it. But instead, David sneaked up very close to Saul and cut off a piece of his robe. To show us David's heart, it was just a little while later when he felt so convicted about it that he wanted to apologize. "...David's heart troubled him..." (1 Sam. 24:5).

He told his men (the ones who had urged him to kill Saul), "I shouldn't have done this and I feel guilty about humiliating the king. I should not have stretched forth my hand, seeing he is the anointed of the Lord."

Even the best of us, at times, have done our "robe cutting." It is almost irresistible! But let not our hearts become hardened to the point where we enjoy it too much.

A few hours later David followed Saul, and when they got to a convenient place, he called out to him and told him what had happened. He said, "I did not kill you because you are the Lord's anointed" (see 1 Sam. 24:10). We cannot emphasize enough the deep, reverential respect David had for the fact that Samuel had anointed Saul, even though it had been many years before, and even though Saul's behavior betrayed that very anointing. *Would to God that the "Sauls" in our lives would have the same respect for us and for the presence of God in our lives.*

Emotional Wreck

Upon being confronted with David's mercy and tender heart, Saul "lifted up his voice and wept" (see 1 Sam. 24:16). And he made many promises, even predicting that David would one day be king. But David was not convinced or tricked by Saul's tears. *Crocodile tears can be turned on and off by people with emotional problems, and cannot always be trusted as a true expression of repentance.* David and his men rose up and went to their hiding place.

On at least one occasion David went to Samuel and told him everything that Saul had done to him (see

1 Sam.. 19:18). What wonderful ministry he must have received from Samuel during these intimate times. I'm sure from reading the Psalms that David broke down and wept before this elderly prophet and found much consolation from him. It may be difficult to think of this Young Warrior ever being in tears. But he often cried. *No one gets to the throne without suffering.* David didn't get to the throne riding in a Cadillac.

How wonderful to have someone who understands! In this day and age when most people are so caught up with the material world, it is very difficult to find someone who knows about cave Adullam and the ragtag army, much less the deep hurts and pain of being persecuted for righteousness' sake. We do need someone to go to—someone who understands. In my lifetime I have had two such people. Shortly after I poured out my soul to them, they each died—first one, and then the other.

At this point in David's life, Samuel died, too. From now on, except for some very short moments with Jonathan, David was on his own. And he had to tell all of his troubles and heartaches to God. And he did. And the Lord listened. And David found himself becoming more and more the man that others needed and sought out. *He became the listening ear, the consoler and encourager of the brethren* (see 1 Thess. 4:18; 5:11; Col. 4:11). *What a tremendous ministry this is in our day and age, and how needed it is!*

I wondered why the Lord took such wonderful men out of my life. Now I know why. He wanted to be that wonderful Man to me, and He wanted me to enter into an even more personal intimacy with Him, until I told Him everything that was in my heart. When you have no one else but God, then you will spill your inner self out to Him. And, of course, this is what He has been waiting for all along. He does want to become our very best Friend! He wants it more than we do.

He also causes us to graduate along our spiritual journey. There are many Young Warriors who need a Samuel to go to. There are many Young Warriors who are almost bewildered and overcome by the circumstances of life. *They need to hear from someone who can say with authority, "I've been through it all. I have been broken and tested beyond all human ability to take it. And I am not only still here, I am victorious!"*

Spear and Water Bottle

On another occasion the Lord caused a deep sleep to fall upon Saul and his soldiers. While they slept, David and Abishai, one of David's brave men, crept into the camp and stole Saul's spear and water bottle. Abishai urged David to kill him. "...Let me strike him at once with the spear, right to the earth; and I will not have to strike him a second time!" (1 Sam. 26:8)

So many of God's people are sound asleep during this exciting hour, just like Saul and his men. Perhaps the Lord has put them to sleep so that they don't get in the way and botch things up. (Notice: David did not pray for them to wake up.) In the meantime, the ragtag team is having adventure after adventure. It is an exciting day for those of us who are awake!

And don't worry about those who are asleep. They will wake up when they find out what they are missing. God is awakening them one by one and selecting those whom He knows will join the new generation of Young Warriors. Why wake up the people who are better off asleep?

But David would not let Abishai kill Saul that night. "The Lord forbid that I should stretch out my hand against the Lord's anointed" (1 Sam. 26:11a).

Crossing to the other side of a ravine for safety, David began yelling to the sleeping troops. Abner, the very man who was responsible for the king's life exclaimed, "Who are you calling out to the king?" (1 Sam. 26:14)

David identified himself and upbraided Abner for not doing his duty. "You should be put to death for sleeping during your watch and not protecting the king."

Then he asked Abner what had happened to Saul's spear and water bottle. All of Saul's men were greatly humiliated. And Saul made yet another promise not to hurt David.

It is interesting that immediately following this promise from the king, David said in his heart, "Now I shall perish someday by the hand of Saul" (1 Sam. 27:1).

So, even brave and valiant David gave into his fears at times. *He fell into the trap that many of us have entered. He began to believe his own thoughts instead of choosing to believe the inner voice of the Spirit of God.*

David fled with his men to Gath and it turned out to be a very wise thing to do (see 1 Sam. 27:2). Saul's attitude had not changed. There could not have been a better place to hide than with the Philistines!

Have You Been to Ziklag?

David's team had now grown into a considerable-sized army; plus the 600 men had their wives and children with them, too. God gave him favor with the king of Gath. And Achish even gave the town of Ziklag to David for him and his troops to live in (see 1 Sam. 27:6). It seemed as though they were safe from trouble, at least temporarily.

But David was very shrewd in his dealing with the Philistines. Pretending to be fighting against his fellow Israelites, he made raid after raid on the Amalekite villages. Because David was so clever, Achish, king of Gath, did not discover what David was doing. In each village David killed every man, woman, and child, so that no one was left alive to take tidings to Gath (see 1 Sam. 27:9).

But many of the military leaders of Gath greatly distrusted David. And when it came time for the all-out war with Israel, they would not allow David and his men to accompany them. They believed that once the battle was raging, David and his men would betray them and attack them. They were keen military strategists.

They reminded Achish that this was the same David about whom the popular song had been sung, "Saul has slain his thousands, and David his ten thousands" (1 Sam. 29:5).

That convinced him and he told David, "I know that you are as good in my sight as an angel of God; neverless the princes of the Philistines have said, 'He shall not go up with us to the battle' " (1 Sam. 29:9). David's life was so exemplary that even the wicked king, Achish, thought of him as an angel. You know that the Lord is shining through your life when even the unsaved people notice it.

It took three days of difficult riding to return to their home in Ziklag, where they had left their women and children. As tough as they were, they must have been very tired when they reached home. To their utter amazement and shock *they found the entire city was burned to the ground and all of their families had been kidnapped!* (see 1 Sam. 30:3)

This was the lowest point in David's life thus far. And it was certainly the lowest point in the life of the ragtag army. It is one thing to have a javelin or two thrown at you. It is quite another thing to have your home burned to the ground and your precious family kidnapped. And it did not happen at a convenient moment. It never does.

Satan seems to know when we are at our very weakest, when we are run down, tired, exhausted, vulnerable. And then, like a snake, he strikes without mercy. It is at moments like these when we are made aware of the depth of his wickedness, and we discover how much he hates Young Warriors. He is seething with anger and jealousy, and he has murder in his heart.

He, too, once knew the thrill of not only being in God's presence, but also being the angel who was "full of wisdom and perfect in beauty" (see Ezek. 28:12). To lose his place with God has made him many times more angry and jealous than Saul ever thought of becoming. Jesus Himself told us that satan has come "to steal, and to kill, and to destroy" (see Jn. 10:10). But we often don't believe it until we encounter something like the depths of Ziklag!

David's men were so completely overwhelmed by this depressing situation that, on top of everything else that David was facing at the moment, they decided to kill him. *His own men wanted to stone him.* These were the very people who had come to him in such a pitiful state: in distress, in debt, and in discontent. And he had taken them in, just as they were, with all of their character flaws and debts. They were now going to show their appreciation by killing him! They had completely lost the vision.

What would you do? What do you do when you are surprised by your Ziklag? *If you are being used by God to do damage to satan's kingdom, then your "Ziklag" will come to you as sure as the grass is green.* Prepare for it. Be ready for it.

The Bible says that David "was greatly distressed for the people spoke of stoning him, because the soul of all the people was grieved, every man for his sons and for his daughters" (1 Sam. 30:6a). There is nothing more dear to us than our offspring, our children, and the ragtag team was placing the full blame upon David's shoulders. (When all else fails: Kill a preacher!) A lesser man would have collapsed under the pressure. Instead, the Bible says that "David strengthened himself in the Lord his God" (1 Sam. 30:6).

Samuel was no longer available for David to consult with. He had been dead for several months. David's parents and relatives were still in Gath and he could not ask his father for advice. Jonathan, his closest friend, at this very moment was receiving his death blow from the Philistine archers (see 1 Sam. 31:2).

David only had God. *Only God!* And it is to Him that David turned. We are not told what David did to encourage himself in God, but it must not have taken him long. Otherwise, he would have been stoned to death by his own men. We, too, must learn how to encourage ourselves in God. There will be times when we will not have weeks and months to leisurely seek the Lord about something. Some decisions must be made on the spur of the moment.

When David emerged from God's presence, he was the commander-in-chief once again. He began giving orders. Speaking to Abiathar, the priest, he said, "Bring me the ephod!" He asked God what to do and God told him to mount up and chase after the Amalekites.

"Pursue, for you shall surely overtake them and without fail recover all" (1 Sam. 30:8).

I can hear David shouting to his ragtags, "Mount up! We are going to find our wives and our children. And we are going to rescue them."

Not one voice was raised in protest. No one resisted. People recognize real authority.

But when they reached the Brook Besor, 200 of the men were so exhausted (Remember: They had already ridden for three days) that they could go no further (see 1 Sam. 30:10). But David and the 400 went further. You will go further than you ever thought humanly possible. And it will not be the flesh and its strength that will sustain you. You will be moving in the supernatural!

David found the Amalekites who had kidnapped his family and burned their homes to the ground. He and his ragtags attacked them by night and killed all but 400 of them, who escaped on camels. And he recovered all that the Amalekites had carried away (see 1 Sam. 30:17-18). *God turned David's biggest nightmare into one of his greatest military achievements. Every Israelite was saved!*

Saul's Death

Finally, in God's sovereign time plan, it was the moment for David to become king. It was time for him to actually sit on the throne, and to enter into the purpose of his anointing. If ever a man had proved himself worthy, David had. Time and time again he had opportunity to kill Saul, but he never lifted his finger against him. He put up with hardship that most of us will never have to endure. He lost his home and was separated from his parents and family members. He lived in a cave and often slept out in the wild places where he was hiding. He had to take food as he found it, and bathe when it was possible. I'm sure that if anyone ever looked like a jungle fighter, David looked the part.

And all of this time he kept faith in his God. Now it was time to be rewarded.

Each of us, too, as God's people, will be rewarded for the work we have performed here on earth for our King. "Finally there is laid up for me the crown of righteousness..." (2 Tim. 4:8).

But before David could be king, Saul had to die. On the battlefield the archers' arrows found their mark, and Saul and his three sons fell.

David was a man after God's own heart and he saw things from God's perspective. Our natural man could rejoice at this moment and point out Saul's wickedness. Instead, David mourned for him and said, "The beauty of Israel is slain. He had been anointed with oil. He and Jonathan were lovely and pleasant in their lives" (see 2 Sam. 1:19,21,23).

For more than ten years Saul had attempted to have David killed. He died with bitterness, hatred, jealousy, resentment, depression, and rage within his heart. And still David called him "lovely" and "pleasant." His words, now God's Words, show us how He looks past all of our faults. Perhaps He looks at us in this way, too—for what we might have been!

Chapter Seven

Jonathan: Yahweh Has Given

*O*ur children are directly affected by how we live our lives. But some children are able, for some unknown reason, to rise above their parents and run past them. Jonathan was such a child. In some strange way it appears that the anointing that was upon Jonathan's father flowed down into his life.

What a wonderful thought that *what we receive from the Lord can be passed on to succeeding generations!* My children can directly benefit from my obedience, prayer, Bible study, and soul-winning. As they watch me going out on adventure after adventure with the Lord, in turn, they will desire this in their lives. But I think that *the key to this is whether they see me enjoying God or simply going through the motions of being religious.* If they see this and think, "Wow! This is the best life anyone could ever wish to have!"—then they will want it, too. "...their heart shall rejoice as if with wine. Yes, *their children shall see it and be glad;* their heart shall rejoice in the Lord" (Zech. 10:7).

In some cases the children have seen "it" and have been bored, totally turned off, or even become God haters. We must have Life ourselves, not just religion. Some of the most bitter young people I have ever met have come from "Christian" homes, some of them from parsonages.

But what a privilege and an honor it is to pass onto our children a rich heritage of faith in God! One thing I have tried to show my children is that serving God is fun—very much fun—and a lot more fun than serving the devil. I have gone out on more than 75 missionary adventures to foreign lands, and I have seen some of the most magnificent places on earth—45 countries so far—and more than 30 trips to Haiti, China, and the Philippines. My children have been privileged to visit places like Mt. Everest, The Great Wall, Kilimanjaro, Kanchenjunga, Tiananmen Square, and South American and African jungles. Two of my children live in Jerusalem. Yes, they have lived the adventure with me! And they know that as a family we have actually done the things that most families can't even dream about doing. *And they know that they are loved.* We joke about the fact that they have "grown up in the Holiday Inn."

Now I watch in amazement as my children go to places that even I have not visited. They are running right past me and I love it. My great joy is watching them as they go forth under their own personal anointing, doing great exploits for God. Actually, as I sit by my wood-burning stove in the mountains, reading and writing, I am fulfilled in my spirit by knowing that *this anointing has been passed on.* They didn't inherit it from me; they each sought the Lord and received it on their own.

I spent many years traveling 100,000 miles each year on airplanes. So travel is no longer the addiction that it once was for me. I get my "highs" in other ways now. I still go out on a caper once in a while, as God directs, but now I am in a more relaxed mode—and rightfully so. I guess that I have shifted down into second gear. I have done my thing (most of it), and now it is time for them to do theirs! And I am more than willing to give them my full support. I love to hear their stories of exploits as they pioneer new works. And I love to hear their new ideas that the Holy Spirit is giving them. These Young Warriors—that is what it is all about!

By God's grace my five daughters are all soul-winners. We have always believed that the best defense is a good offense. So if I have any advice for parents, it is to pray that God's anointing be upon their children—and then *allow them to become anything that they want to become.*

We have so many hilarious stories from our travels that we could fill a book with them. One incident pops into mind:

Bryan and Konda spent a month in China doing missionary work. Knowing the value of spreading the gospel, they took $5,000 out of their personal savings account and took off to see how the Lord would use them. And He did use them mightily.

They were on a bus somewhere near Beijing and another family from South America was on the bus with them. Suddenly the man asked Bryan, "What are you doing in China? Why have you come here?"

There was something in the man's voice that Bryan detected, and he knew instantly in his spirit that the man was a believer. He knew that he could be trusted.

He answered, "We are here for a month giving Bibles to the Chinese people."

"Bibles!" the man's wife exclaimed. "We're Christians, too. And I know a man from the United States who brings teams of people to China twice a year. I have heard him speak at Blue Mountain Christian Retreat in Pennsylvania. He is the director of Bibles to China and his name is Wesley Smith. Have you ever heard of him?"

"Sure. We've heard of him," my kids laughed. "He's our Dad!"

The man handed them his business card later with the comment, "If you ever need a job or want to visit us in South America, here's our address and telephone number."

Later, when they read the business card, they were amazed to discover that the man on the bus was the vice president of Citibank! The Lord has His own sense of humor and ways of causing His people to "connect."

Usually the concept of generational transference is explored in all of the negative aspects: alcoholism, drug addiction, sexual promiscuity, child and wife abuse, etc. We become so careful and paranoid about passing our faults onto our children, that *we overlook the awesome power of God to impart to them the positive qualities from our lives.*

With the Holy Spirit and the anointing, I believe that the Lord covers a multitude of sins in terms of this generational transference. This is nowhere more obvious and glaring than in Jonathan's precious life. We might do better praying that God would pass onto our children the anointing, gifts, and good things that are in our personalities, rather than worrying ourselves sick that our children might be like we are. Here it is again—releasing them to God!

Jonathan should have been the mean kid on the block, who could in an instant change from a normal person to an enraged killer. But he was not. He should have been proud, arrogant, selfish, paranoid, fearful, and deeply affected by the fact that his father dabbled in the occult.

The Bible first mentions Jonathan as being in charge of 1,000 soldiers in Gibeah (see 1 Sam. 13:2). Later in that chapter the Bible identifies him as being Saul's son (see 1 Sam. 13:16). As commander of 1,000 soldiers, Jonathan had the great opportunity to go out on adventures for the Lord, for his father, and for his country. The very first raid he made was on the garrison of the Philistines in Geba (see 1 Sam. 13:3). The Bible doesn't tell us any details, but it is very clear that Jonathan and his men slew the Philistines there and won a wonderful victory.

It was the kind of victory that God's people needed at that moment. Saul recognized this and declared that the "Hebrews hear" about it by blowing the trumpet and announcing what had happened. The Bible says, "Saul blew the trumpet throughout all the land" (see 1 Sam. 13:3).

But the announcement was somewhat different from the actual event! What the people ended up hearing was that Saul had smitten the garrison of the Philistines, not his son, Jonathan. Saul was only too eager to receive credit for this victory.

It is obvious from observing this that there was a vast difference between the son and father: "Jonathan slew and Saul blew." There are a lot of people today who are good at talking Christianity, but the real warriors are those who are going out and getting the job done. Jonathan did not seem to care who got the credit for it. *He derived his pleasure from actually conquering the enemy.*

On another occasion, just out of the blue, Jonathan told his armor-bearer, "Let's go over to the Philistine garrison" (see 1 Sam. 14:6).

This was a spontaneous thought and a spontaneous act. There are times when the Holy Spirit will put something in our minds that just has to be done now—like yesterday. This was one of those times in Jonathan's life.

The feeling inside of him was so urgent that he did not take time to tell his father about it. There just wasn't time for a committee meeting. He and his armor-bearer set out immediately. No one knew that they had left the camp or what they were up to.

Jonathan had a further burst of faith and he told his armor-bearer, "...It may be that the Lord will work for us. For nothing restrains the Lord from saving by many or by few" (1 Sam. 14:6).

He decided to lay out a fleece in order for them to find clear direction. "If the Philistines say, 'Stay there and we will come to you,' then we will stay where we are, and not go up to them. But if they say, 'Come up to where we are,' then we will go up, knowing that the Lord has delivered them into our hand. This will be our sign."

So when they approached the Philistine garrison, they purposely allowed the enemies to see them. The Philistines made a big joke out of their arrival because the rest of the Israelites were hiding themselves, instead of fighting.

Playing right into Jonathan's fleece, they said, "Come up to us, and we will show you something" (see 1 Sam. 14:12). Little did they realize that Jonathan and his armor-bearer would show them "something."

These next few verses need to be read very slowly (see 1 Sam. 14:13-16). Jonathan climbed up the rocks first. In the natural it would seem that the 20 armed soldiers up on top of the hill could have easily killed the two of them.

But something very strange took place. As Jonathan moved forward, crawling on his hands, the soldiers "fell" before him. Then his armor-bearer proceeded to kill all 20 of them.

(It appears that the Philistine soldiers fell down under a strange power in a similar manner as the crowd was "slain" who came out to arrest Jesus (see Jn. 18:6). If you recall the story, it was the night before Jesus was to be crucified. The crowd had come with weapons to arrest Him and had said, "We are looking for Jesus of Nazareth." Jesus had simply replied, "I'm Jesus!" When He said that, the entire crowd went backward, and fell to the ground.)

So Jonathan's armor-bearer had a pretty easy job. The 20 Philistine soldiers were already "slain," lying on the ground, and all that he had to do was come along with his sword and kill them. It is very obvious that this was a supernatural victory—God was honoring Jonathan's inspirational faith.

(Almost every believer knows the story of David and Goliath because it was told in such great detail. And it is one of the great stories of the Bible. However, although Goliath was a huge man—a giant—David really just killed one man. Jonathan and his armor-bearer killed 20 men!)

Then the earth quaked so violently that the entire Philistine army became confused and terrified and they began killing each other. It was like a domino effect (see 1 Sam. 14:15-16). Once the 20 were disposed of, then great fear gripped the hearts of the Philistine soldiers. Some of Saul's scouts were watching this in amazement as they saw the entire Philistine army flee away.

What a lesson for us today! Greater things may be accomplished than we even know about when we obey the Lord in "little" things. The effect is like throwing a stone into a calm lake. The ripples continue to expand, even after the rock has been thrown. In this instance, with Jonathan and his armor-bearer, instead of ripples it was an earthquake. Our obedience does have lasting and eternal consequences! It may seem at times that the Lord inspires us to do something "small," but later He may cause something greater to come of it.

Saul knew nothing about what his son had accomplished, and he was in a planning meeting at the time, trying to find out what kind of military strategy to use against the Philistines (see 1 Sam. 14:18-19). But the war had already been won! What mighty accomplishments Young Warriors perform as they are led and inspired by the Holy Spirit!

After this incident David came on the scene and slew Goliath. Jonathan was right there to observe. Immediately, something in him wanted to become friends with David. They were of kindred spirits. The same Spirit was in both of them.

So they became friends. "...The soul of Jonathan was knit to the soul of David, and Jonathan loved him as his own soul" (1 Sam. 18:1). By giving David his princely robe, clothing, and weapons, he relinquished his right to the throne! So this was not just any old shallow friendship. Jonathan was not only laying down his life for David, he also was laying down his future.

This was not an ordinary friendship. This was spirit to spirit, soul to soul. Their friendship became so deep that David later described it this way: "...your love to me was wonderful, surpassing the love of women" (2 Sam. 1:26). And David certainly did not lack in his love toward the opposite sex.

From this point forward Jonathan was torn between his friendship with David and his loyalty to his father. And the more angry and jealous Saul became, the more difficult it was for Jonathan. If you have ever been in a position where you love two people, and the two of them cannot get along, then you can appreciate how Jonathan must have felt.

The pain must have peaked when his father actually asked him to murder David (see 1 Sam. 20:31). How do you kill your best friend? How do you assassinate someone with whom you have made a covenant? Saul was asking the impossible from his young son. Saul was asking him to violate everything sacred within him. *He was asking him to blatantly disobey the Spirit's voice within his life.* He was ordering him to trample and desecrate the One who had given him the supernatural victory over the Philistines.

Jonathan did what any Young Warrior would do. He told David about his father's plans. Then he took it a step further and pled with his father on David's behalf. This could have cost him his life. A Young Warrior is willing to risk everything for the Truth.

Jonathan's efforts were short-lived. Saul was temporarily pacified, and brought David back as his anointed music man—his personal exorcist. But within days the evil spirit from God came upon Saul and he tried the old javelin thing again. It was the straw that broke the camel's back. David left and never returned.

Jonathan and David met secretly after that. He told David that he knew everything that his father planned, and that he would make every effort to save his life (see 1 Sam. 20:1-42). *He did not know that the very next day this effort would almost cost him his life.*

He was at the dinner table with his father when suddenly Saul asked, "Where is David?"

Jonathan replied, "David asked permission to go visit his family in Bethlehem, and I told him that he could go. I guess his brother put a lot of pressure on him to be there. That's why he is not here."

When he said that, his father became so angry that he began cursing Jonathan and his mother. We pretty much know what that language would sound like without getting too explicit (see 1 Sam. 20:30).

Then he ordered Jonathan to arrest David and bring him to him so that he could kill him. Jonathan was being pushed to the limit and he replied, "What do you want to kill him for? What has he done?"

Saul's anger once again became so out of control that he picked up his javelin and threw it at Jonathan. Fortunately, Jonathan was not killed. But he did show a side of his personality that we only see here. "So Jonathan arose from the table in fierce anger..." (1 Sam. 20:34).

Today there is a lot of talk about child abuse and the adverse effect that it has upon someone's personality. Thousands of people are suffering internally from parental sexual, emotional, verbal, and physical abuse. Many people, seemingly, cannot get over it. *And not only do they not get over it, they also repeat to their children and spouses what they saw and what was maliciously done to them. They become what they hate.*

Somehow Jonathan remained free from this cycle. I believe that it was because of his wonderful relationship with the Lord that he was freed from the sins that tormented his father. A man I know told me, "Because of what I experienced when I was young, I should have become a serial killer. If anyone had an excuse, I did."

Instead, this man is one of the finest husbands and fathers that you could find anywhere in America. And his wife, children, and grandchildren prove it. You do know a tree by its fruit (see Mt. 7:16).

The Young Warrior, Jonathan, was not only victorious fighting with the Philistines; he was victorious in his personal life, too.

David owed his very life to Jonathan. Even though David was running for his life, Jonathan would periodically meet with him secretly to bring him encouragement. The last time that they met is recorded in First Samuel 23. After this they would never see each other in this life again.

Jonathan "strengthened his hand in God" (1 Sam. 23:16), and even prophesied to David that he would be the king over Israel. That part of the prophecy was accurate, but he also told him that he would serve "next to him."

(Some Bible scholars believe that even this part of Jonathan's prophecy will come true after David is "resurrected in the latter days" and sits as literal king over both houses of Israel, as he did before, while alive on earth. Some scholars think that David and Jonathan will be the two witnesses in Revelation. Others think it will be Enoch and Elijah. (Compare: Revelation 3:7; Isaiah 22:22; Acts 15:16; Amos 9:11; Hosea 3:5; Jeremiah 30:9; Ezekiel 34:24, 37:24-25; Acts 13:22; Zechariah 12:10; Isaiah 9:7, 37:35, 55:3; Psalm 132:11.)

But because of the ties he had to his father, Jonathan would not live to see that day, or to experience the joy of serving his friend when he became commander-in-chief. How powerful the two of them could have been together!

Somehow, even though he was the prince, Jonathan knew that the anointing upon David's life would carry him beyond his own rightful appointment to the throne. He knew that David would be king. And he was more than willing to relinquish his position to David.

There are not many "Jonathans" around these days. But every leader surely needs a friend like this.

The closing scene in Jonathan's life is heartbreaking. Jonathan and his two brothers were at their father's side, in yet another battle with the Philistines. On Mount Gilboa "...the Philistines killed Jonathan, Abinadab, and Malchishua, Saul's sons" (1 Sam. 31:2).

We could think about what might have been. But, really, it could not have been, and it was not meant to be. *As we know the character of Jonathan, he could not have been anywhere except at his father's side.* In spite of who Saul was, Jonathan loved him. Someone has said, and rightfully so, "Blood is thicker than water." It is certainly true in Jonathan's story. In his heart he would have loved to have been by David's side in Ziklag when he needed him so desperately. He would have loved to have moved in the spirit with his covenant friend, enjoying the adventures that Young Warriors are supposed to experience.

Yes, in his heart he would have loved to be doing many other things. But he was faithful to his father until the very end; and then he made the supreme sacrifice, showing once again, his willingness to lay down his life. If any Bible figure was a type of Christ, surely it was Jonathan. As was mentioned before, there are not many "Jonathans." He was very pleasant, swifter than an eagle, and stronger than a lion (see 2 Sam. 1:23).

Not only did Jonathan meet an untimely death because of his loyalty and faithfulness to his father, but his body was also desecrated. When the Philistines came to strip the dead bodies, they found his body, the bodies of his two brothers, and Saul's body. The Philistines wanted to make a statement with this victory. So they dismembered the bodies and took them to Beth-shan. There they hung the headless corpses on the wall for everyone to see. This was an utter humiliation for all of Israel, to have their king's body and the bodies of his three princes strung up like meat in the marketplace (see 1 Sam. 31:8-10).

When the men of Jabesh-gilead learned about the desecration of the corpses, as one man they arose and traveled all night to Beth-shan. We are not told what took place when they arrived at this Philistine stronghold, but the Bible makes it clear that they returned with all four bodies. I'm sure that the Philistines did not just let them take the bodies. Either they craftily stole them, or there was a struggle. Whatever took place, we know that they succeeded in their efforts (see 1 Sam. 31:11-12).

One reason that the men of Jabesh-gilead put forth so much effort in returning the bodies to Israel is because they felt that they owed Saul something. Back in chapter 11 we find the account of Nahash, the Ammonite, threatening the men of Jabesh. They could either fight with the Ammonites, or surrender. The condition of surrender was that every man would have his right eye gouged out by Nahash. When Saul heard about this situation (before he had grieved the Lord out of his life) the Spirit of God came upon him and he rallied 330,000 troops to the rescue. That day they slew thousands of Ammonites, and the people of Jabesh were saved from entering into a horrible covenant with the enemy.

How satan desires to hinder our sight! If he can just keep us from seeing spiritual Truth, then he has accomplished his purpose. He knows that if we begin to see the Truth that God is revealing in these last days, then we will rise up and become the kind of Young Warriors who will be a real threat to him. We must keep both of our spiritual eyes open! This is certainly not the time to compromise and attempt to become as much like the world as we can. The Church is on a suicide run whenever it looks to the world for direction, whether it be in attitude, message content, music, or whatever.

Praise the Lord for those, like Saul in chapter 11, who are rescuing God's people from destruction and humiliation. *One of the most valuable ministries today in America is to save the Christians from their impending doom—of life without meaning, filled with boredom and purposelessness.*

So the men of Jabesh returned the bodies of Saul and his three sons to their town. Because the bodies were dismembered and mutilated, there was nothing else for them to do but to burn them. The burning process was probably an attempt to erase the stigma of the bodies having been offered to the Philistine god Ashtaroth. Then they took the bones and buried them under a tree in Jabesh.

But that was not all that the valiant men of Jabesh did. Israel had just experienced the worst defeat in their history. Thousands of soldiers had been killed by the Philistines, and now they did not even have a king. So the *men of Jabesh fasted seven days* (1 Sam. 31:13). This fast changed Israel's history. These men were farmers who had to work hard every day, but they fasted for a full week. This was not just in sorrow for their slain king and his three sons—*they were fasting and praying for their national survival and future.*

You might say that God already had things under control anyway. Why did they need to deny themselves for an entire week? Prayer is a very interesting experience. Prayer is not logical. But many things in life are not logical. Why pray to a God who already knows the future and will carry out His purposes—regardless?

The best explanation that I can come up with is that God has chosen to work through prayer. Yes, *He knows the end from the beginning, but our prayers cause Him to make certain decisions.* "The effective fervent prayer of a righteous man avails much" (Jas. 5:16b). Elijah prayed that it would not rain, and it did not rain on the earth for three and one half years. Then, he prayed again, and the heavens gave rain (see Jas. 5:17-18).

Would this have happened whether he prayed or didn't pray? No one can answer this question, but *one of the greatest faith-builders for Young Warriors is to see prayers answered!* I'm sure that the men of Jabesh-gilead rejoiced more than any of the other Israelites when David was crowned king. They knew then that their prayers and fasting had been seen by God and He had turned the utter defeat by the Philistines into a glorious victory.

David, after he became king, also gave them special recognition for their brave deeds. Then he pronounced a blessing upon them and rewarded them (see 2 Sam. 2:5-6).

When all else fails, Young Warriors fast and pray. Then God moves mountains and giants are slain. Sometimes a nation is even changed!

Chapter Eight

The Young Warrior

*M*odern America has substituted many things in place of the anointing. The Young Warrior wants no part of that. He is not interested in paving parking lots, putting up huge air-conditioned halls of worship, plastering his name in advertising campaigns, or wandering aimlessly around at the mall. Tens of thousands of Young Warriors are obeying the voice of the Holy Spirit and are accomplishing great things for God. Some of these Young Warriors get more done during one missionary adventure than some organizations accomplish in a lifetime.

The key strategy for the Young Warrior is remaining still until he hears the voice of his Father. Then he moves into action faster than you can blink your eye—whether it is to visit a neighbor or ride a jetliner to the other side of the world. It doesn't matter to him. He only wants to serve, and be excellent in what he does. The rewards will come later. And he does not need to be rewarded by man. His God will reward him in ways that no organization or group of men could ever reward him (see Mt. 6:18; Mk. 9:41; Lk. 6:35; 1 Cor. 3:8,14; 9:17; Col. 3:24; 1 Tim. 5:18). And he knows this from experience.

He knows that he will walk on the high places of the earth, where most men only dream of walking (see Deut. 28:1). His Father has told him that he will receive anything that he asks for in Jesus' name (see Jn. 14:14; 15:16; 16:23-24,26). But the Young Warrior only wants to ask according to his Father's will. He is as content herding sheep on a hillside as he is galloping ahead of an army through a valley.

He knows that his heavenly Father knows ahead of time what he needs and wants, and He usually gives it to him even before he thinks to ask (see Ps. 91:15; Is. 65:24; Jer. 33:3). He knows from personal experience that his God heals, delivers, and saves to the uttermost. He knows that wherever he goes his God will be with him. He knows that his God sends angels ahead of him to prepare the way (see Deut. 1:30; Is. 52:12; Heb. 1:14). He knows that no man can stand before him all the days of his life (see Josh. 1:5). He knows that every place where the sole of his foot treads, has been given to him by God (see Josh 1:3).

He knows that as God was with Moses, so will He be with the Young Warrior (see Josh 1:5). He knows that he will prosper wherever he goes. He knows that he will make his own way prosperous, and that he will have good success (see Josh. 1:8). He knows that he will be blessed in the city. He knows that he will be blessed in the country (see Deut. 28:3). He knows that his basket and store are blessed (see Deut. 28:5). He knows that the fruit of his body is blessed (see Deut. 28:4). He knows that his enemies will be smitten by the Lord before his face. He knows that his enemies will come out against him one way, and flee before him seven ways (see Deut. 28:7). He knows that the Lord has commanded the blessing upon him in everything that he does (see Deut. 28:8). He knows that the Lord is establishing him as a holy person unto Himself (see Deut. 28:9). He knows that all the people of the earth will see that he is called by the name of the Lord. He knows that even kings and rulers will be afraid of him (see Deut. 28:10).

He knows that the Lord will make him rich in goods and in the fruit of his body. He knows that the Lord will open to him of His good treasure (see Deut. 28:11-12). He knows that the Lord will open the windows of Heaven and pour out a blessing and there won't even be room for it all (see Mal. 3:10). He knows that he will lend to the nations and not borrow (see Deut. 28:12). He knows the Lord will make him the head and not the tail (see Deut. 28:13). He knows that he will be above and not beneath. And he knows that Jesus will never leave him or forsake him (see Mt. 28:20).

No! The Young Warrior has no desire to trade his calling for anything that the secular or religious world system has to offer. He feels sorry for both the secular and religious community for not understanding and entering into what the Lord has for them. The Young Warrior would not trade places with anyone he has ever met. He does not envy anyone. He is not jealous of them. Instead, he prays for them. He attempts, at times, to soothe their tormented minds and spirits. But he will not walk their walk or try to function in their armor. It has never done them any good, and he knows that it certainly won't do him any good.

In fact, he can't even take one step wearing their armor. The Young Warrior must be free to carry a picnic basket or to slay a giant. He must always remain vigilant and available to his Father's beckoning. As a result, he cannot become entangled in this world (see Gal. 5:1; 2 Tim. 2:4). His affairs must be in such order that he can leave the sheep with a keeper on a moment's notice and go off on a new adventure.

The Young Warrior cannot live like everyone else lives. If he did, then he would accomplish the same things they accomplish. His life must be different. He is in this world, but not of it (see Jn. 17:16). He is seated with Christ in heavenly places (see Eph. 1:3; 2:6), and he constantly has a picture of eternity in his mind.

He is motivated by his heavenly vision. So when he receives the Macedonian call, he is up early the next morning to accomplish his mission. He doesn't "fight with God" for 30 years before he "enters the ministry."

When the Lord says, "Jump," the Young Warrior says, "How high?" He is eager to be about his Father's business!

When tragedy and trouble come, the Young Warrior takes it in stride. He knows that nothing comes into his life that is not ordered by his Owner. *He knows that he was bought and purchased by God's Son's blood* (see Acts 20:28). He knows this was an extremely high price that was paid for him. He knows that it was the highest price that could ever be paid for anything or anyone—in Heaven or on earth.

So he knows that he is God's property. He belongs to God. He knows that he is the son of a King. He knows that his Father is the King. The Young Warrior knows that he is not his own (see 1 Cor. 6:19-20; 7:23), and he knows that God takes good care of His property.

So when heartache comes, he feels it like anyone else feels it. He weeps; he cries; and sometimes the pain is so intense that he even howls. But underneath it all he knows that there is a foundation that is unshakable. He knows that the Chief Cornerstone in his life is the Lord Jesus Christ. And he knows that "the Chief" has experienced more than he will ever experience. He knows that the heartache and trouble that his Owner has gone through makes anything he goes through seem pale in comparison.

He knows that the One he serves has been despised and rejected. So he learns to expect it himself. And when it happens, he talks to his "Samuel" about it. When the Young Warrior becomes despondent, he knows that the One who gave him the anointing is well acquainted with grief and sorrow. When people become filled with jealousy and envy because of his walk with God, he remembers that Jesus was despised and rejected of men.

When his grief is too much to bear, and he finds himself in burned-out "Ziklag," then he encourages himself in his God. It is then that he remembers that his God has already borne his grief, and carried his sorrows.

When the Young Warrior recalls that the Son of God came down from outer space to planet earth for the express purpose of being wounded for his transgressions, it comforts him and causes him to love his Creator all the more. When he thinks about the Son of Man being bruised for his iniquities, it makes him thankful beyond words. And he knows that there is healing from His stripes—any kind of healing that he needs.

He knows that when his Master was afflicted and oppressed, He did not open His mouth. And he is reminded not to defile himself, either, even if this leads to martyrdom. He remembers that He made His grave with the wicked. He remembers that the Mighty Warrior of Heaven participated in no violence. And when he is tempted to lie, he recalls that the Faithful and True Witness never had deceit in His mouth.

And he knows that God will divide him a portion with the great—that He will divide the spoil with the strong. The Young Warrior knows that if he pours out his soul, even unto death, that the grave has no victory over him. He knows that even death has no power over him. And he knows that it is not because of who he is, but it is because of the anointing that he has received. He knows that his God never forgets anything—especially the anointing. And he knows that even in death there is life and resurrection. The Young Warrior knows that there is Life beyond the grave (see Is. 53).

The Young Warrior knows that this is what he has lived for. He knows that there is actually a place where all of the Warriors before him have gone. He is excited about the certainty of seeing them, of being with them, and of listening to them tell their adventures to him face-to-face. He expects to be able to tell his stories, too, in an atmosphere where there is perfect belief and rejoicing.

The Young Warrior will continue forward no matter what happens. Kingdoms may come and kingdoms may go. But he knows that he has been promised an eternal home. And he has been promised that in his Father's house are many mansions. He knows that Jesus has gone before him to prepare a place especially for him. He knows that He will come and receive him unto Himself, because the King wants him to be with Him forever (see Jn. 14:1-3).

So the Young Warrior remains motivated and looks forward to the next assignment. And he knows that regardless of his earthly age, he will always be a Young Warrior!

Epilogue

Do You Want to Be Anointed?

*H*ave you read enough? Are you hungry and eager to participate in the most exciting and fulfilling lifestyle available today? If so, I will explain to you, very simply, how you can receive this anointing.

First of all, let's get something clear. We live in a culture where most things are done very quickly. We go through the drive-thru to get our money and our food. We put change in a machine and out comes the candy or soda. We have come to expect to get what we want when we want it. All of this convenience is great, but it tends to spoil us somewhat. Do not expect to say a 15-second prayer and then head back to your television set—not if you plan to receive something so sacred as the anointing of the Holy Spirit. (There has just been too much flippancy and shallowness connected with

American Christianity. So I felt that I had to say that first.)

God does not function in a way that is limited by our culture or lifestyle. He has His own lifestyle and cannot be intimidated one bit by us earthlings. However, He will respond to you if you are sincere and honest, deep in your heart.

The first thing that we need to understand is that there are no "Samuels" around today to come to you with a horn filled with oil and pour it upon your head. So don't look for one or wait for one. Man is not the one who anoints today!

Jesus Christ is the "Anointed One." In other words, He is the One with the anointing, and the One who does the anointing. He is the One who does the anointing today, and no one else. There may be some wonderful preachers around, but only Jesus has the power to pour the heavenly oil upon you.

So it is to Him that we go with our request. The Scripture makes it very clear that "There is one God, and one mediator between God and men, the man Christ Jesus" (1 Tim. 2:5).

How do we know that we should go to Him with our request to receive the anointing? Again, the Scripture makes it crystal clear: "He [Jesus] will baptize you with the Holy Spirit and fire" (Lk. 3:16b).

Step One

So what do we say to Him? It is so very simple. You don't even have to know how to say "long prayers." Just say, "Jesus, please baptize me with the Holy Spirit."

If you are at the table and you want the bread, you say, "Please pass the bread." Then someone passes it to you. When you say to Jesus, "Please baptize me with the Holy Spirit," immediately He baptizes you, whether you feel anything or not. He always answers this prayer!

Again, how do we know this? Jesus Himself, when He was teaching on this subject said, "Everyone who asks, receives" (Lk. 11:10). *Every one!* That certainly includes you. Notice also that He did not say "will receive." He makes it clear that it is immediate.

What is the next sensible thing to do when someone gives you something that you have asked for? You say, "Thank you."

So the next thing that you say to Jesus is: "Thank you, Jesus, for baptizing me with the Holy Spirit."

There you have it. Isn't it simple and easy to understand? It sure is. And *one of the reasons it has to be simple is that people all over the world need to be able to understand this—even people who cannot read or write.* Anyone, anywhere, can pray this prayer and give thanks!

Step Two

Now here is the important one! Do not immediately turn on your television set. I keep emphasizing this and repeating this point because *I believe that television addiction is one of the greatest hindrances to entering into God's purposes.* Instead, open your Bible. Begin at the beginning of any book in the Bible. The Bible is the only book that I know of where people just flip it open and start reading. Some people "study" their Bibles like this for a lifetime and never begin to understand what God is saying. We must read intelligently—from the beginning of each book to the end!

There are 66 books in the Bible and they are all good. Pick any one of them that you feel interested in, and study it. The Bible is all good. This is God's Word directly to you.

In addition to your Bible, have a notebook and pen right beside you. As you read, any verse or thought that is especially interesting to you, write it down. Just as the Scribes of old copied the Bible, *something very powerful takes place within your spirit when you actually write Bible verses.* You must continue to do this day after day. Don't attempt to be religious about it; just study it.

Proceed through each book of the Bible like this, and God will begin speaking to you. Don't worry about the time. God is not timing you to see how long you spend in your "daily devotions." Forget all about that religious stuff. Think, pause, pray, listen, and write! Remember: You are attempting to communicate with the same God that Hannah, Samuel, David, and Jonathan communed with. Listen and watch for the surprising ways He will speak directly to you.

When I began my spiritual journey more than 30 years ago, I became so interested in what I was reading that I spent approximately four to six hours each day studying the Scriptures. But that was me. Don't let that scare you. You do it your way—any way and any time of day, and for any length of time that is comfortable for you. Don't try to wear any one else's armor. Just remember: *The more of the Bible that you get into your spirit, the better you will become acquainted with God. And this is how your faith grows.* If you want faith, don't pray for it, read the Bible. It will automatically come. And God can always be found in His Word.

I did my studying each afternoon and evening when I came home from my teaching job. I would read and write until got tired, and then I would get up and take a long walk outside. Then I would return to my apartment and continue on with my reading.

I still do the same thing now over 30 years later. This is what works for me. I walk one mile up to the top of the mountain, and then one mile back down to our house. This refreshes me and is also good for me physically. I usually talk with God during my walk about some of the things He has been teaching me out of the Bible. It is exhilarating.

When I first began my Bible study, I had my smokes and beer right along with the study. How strange—the Bible stayed and the other two dropped out of my life, but not because of religion or trying. I simply lost the desire. It is somewhat similar to eating boiled cabbage all of your life, and then tasting steak. It really isn't a difficult choice.

After about three months of this, some strange and wonderful things began happening to me. God did speak to me! And it was awesome. I was very excited about what I was finding in the Scriptures. (Till this day I am still excited—except now I am even more excited about it than I was 30 years ago because I know that I am in for surprise after surprise.)

This thing really works.

At that time I was a teacher at a public high school in Flint, Michigan. It was a big inner-city school. I began telling my students what was taking place in my life. So they started coming to my apartment after school. We ate pizza, drank Coke, and studied the Bible together. It was very exciting.

At that time I was a bachelor, so I had a lot of time on my hands. I spent many hours with these young people. I was only a few years older than they were. We would sit around my apartment and they would tell me their stories. We laughed so much. And each day I would tell them one Bible story. I also told them to tell that story, in their own words, to some of their friends at school the next day.

My apartment became so crowded that we had to go into the church across the street. (My apartment was upstairs and the people below me were very relieved when all of these black-jacketed teens quit coming en masse to my home.) After a few months we got kicked out of the church because "black" people were coming to our meetings. Also, the leaders of the church informed me that most of these kids were undesirables— low life. They didn't want them in their building—sinner types, you know.

We didn't make a fuss. We just left. Jesus never stayed where He wasn't wanted. (By the way, that church now has a black pastor and the entire congregation is black. Hmmm!)

We then rented a store-front building right smack in between the black and white communities. Little did I know that one year later God would ask me to quit my job as a schoolteacher. My days at the sheepcote came to an end and I started a journey that has taken me to many parts of the world.

As I look back, one of the main things that I am so thankful for is that I obeyed His invitation. I could have stayed in the secure job that I had, and I am sure that He would have blessed me there, too. But I would have missed so very much.

So get in the Bible and listen for His voice in your life. Don't tell Him what He can or cannot do. He can do anything that He wants to do. He is God! He is not limited by your doctrinal positions. Sometimes He will absolutely astonish you and take your breath away. He is, after all, the God of surprises.

The more you dig into the Bible, the more faith you will have. D.L. Moody put it this way: "I used to pray for faith, and thought that some day faith would come down and strike me like lightning. But faith did not seem to come. Then I began to study God's Word, and faith has been growing ever since."

Yes, the key to this whole thing is taking time and making this the number one priority in your life. If you are serious about being used during this endtime, then you will spend the time and do whatever it takes to make it happen. You must make this a priority above everything else.

I remember so clearly when I first started studying the Bible. My drinking buddies came up to my apartment and wanted me to go party with them. I told them that I didn't have time—I was reading the Bible. You should have seen the looks on their faces! I wasn't trying to be religious or anything. I just wanted to study God's Word. My buddies poured a full bottle of beer over my head and said, "Hey, man, let's get with the program."

I often laugh about that experience. I was anointed with beer instead of oil. And, believe me, I have "gotten with the program"!

When I told them that my desires had completely changed, and so had my lifestyle, they dropped out of my life fast. Now I have friends in many parts of the world who invite me to their homes. I have so many invitations that I cannot possibly go to all of the places. Plus, I am slowing down a little at the young age of 60. I am still a Young Warrior, but I have shifted down into second gear.

Don't even try to convince me that this is a bunch of malarkey. This anointing is real stuff and it has worked so well for our family that we wouldn't trade it for anything that this world has to offer.

So...let's get with the program—God's program. Ask Him to baptize you with the Holy Spirit, and then study your Bible like you really mean it. And if you mean it, He will mean it, too.

He will give you the desires of your heart. But don't expect the "candy" to jump out of the machine instantly. Give it time. It might take a few weeks or months before you start noticing a difference. But when He sees that you are really serious, and not just trying to run some religious thing on Him, He will meet you beyond your expectations. We are talking about the living God of the universe—the same God who reveals Himself in the Bible.

So let's get started. Get your Bible open and get your pen and notebook.

And if I can encourage you, please get in touch. But better yet, get in touch with Him. He can do more for you than I can ever do. However, if you choose to become a Young Warrior, I would love to hear about it.

Some Bible Verses to Help in Your Study

(Note: These verses are taken from the King James Version of the Bible.)

That if thou shalt confess with Thy mouth the Lord Jesus, and shalt believe in Thine heart that God hath raised him from the dead, thou shalt be saved (Romans 10:9).

Jesus Is the Baptizer

John answered, saying unto them all, I indeed baptize you with water; but one mightier than I cometh, the latchet of whose shoes I am not worthy to unloose: He shall baptize you with the Holy Ghost and with fire (Luke 3:16).

(Isn't it interesting that most of us know John 3:16, but we overlook Luke 3:16?)

The New Wine Is Better
(Wine and oil represent the Holy Spirit.)

...Every man at the beginning doth set forth good wine; and when men have well drunk, then that which is worse: but Thou has kept the good wine until now (John 2:10).

Neither do men put new wine into old bottles: else the bottles break, and the wine runneth out, and the bottles perish: but they put new wine into new bottles, and both are preserved (Matthew 9:17).

...These men are full of new wine (Acts 2:13).

...their heart shall rejoice as through wine: yea, their children shall see it, and be glad; their heart shall rejoice in the Lord (Zechariah 10:7).

...I will prophesy unto thee of wine... (Micah 2:11).

Awake, you drunkards, and weep; and howl, all ye drinkers of wine, because of the new wine, for it is cut off from your mouth (Joel 1:5).

...the wine that they should drink (Daniel 1:16).

Stay yourselves, and wonder; cry ye out, and cry: they are drunken, but not with wine; they stagger, but not with strong drink (Isaiah 29:9).

And I will give them one heart, and I will put a new spirit within you; and I will take the stony heart out of their flesh, and will give them an heart of flesh (Ezekiel 11:19).

For John truly baptized with water; but ye shall be baptized with the Holy Ghost not many days hence (Acts 1:5).

But ye shall receive power, after that the Holy Ghost is come upon you: and ye shall be witnesses... (Acts 1:8).

And they were all filled with the Holy Ghost, and began to speak with other tongues, as the Spirit gave them utterance (Acts 2:4).

Then Peter said unto them, Repent, and be baptized every one of you in the name of Jesus Christ for the remission of sins, and ye shall receive the gift of the Holy Ghost. For the promise is unto you, and to your children, and to all that are afar off, even as many as the Lord our God shall call (Acts 2:38-39).

And when they had prayed, the place was shaken where they were assembled together; and they were all filled with the Holy Ghost, and they spake the Word of God with boldness (Acts 4:31).

Now when the apostles which were at Jerusalem heard that Samaria had received the word of God, they sent unto them Peter and John: who, when they were come down, prayed for them, that they might receive the Holy Ghost: (For as yet he was fallen upon none of them: only they were baptized in the name of the Lord Jesus.) Then they laid their hands on them, and they received the Holy Ghost (Acts 8:14-17).

And Ananias went his way, and entered into the house; and putting his hands on him said, Brother Saul, the Lord, even Jesus, that appeared unto thee in the way as thou camest hath sent me, that thou mightest receive thy sight, and be filled with the Holy Ghost (Acts 9:17).

(Even the apostle Paul, who could speak five languages and was very well educated, received the baptism of the Holy Spirit.)

Even Jesus Was Baptized With the Holy Spirit!

Now when all the people were baptized, it came to pass, that Jesus also being baptized, and praying, the heaven was opened, and the Holy Ghost descended in a bodily shape like a dove upon Him, and a voice came from heaven, which said Thou art my beloved Son; in Thee I am well pleased (Luke 3:21-22).

(Wow! If Jesus needed it, and the apostle Paul needed it, do you think that we need it?)

While Peter yet spake these words, the Holy Ghost fell on all them which heard the word. And they of the circumcision which believed were astonished, as many as came with Peter, because that on the Gentiles also was poured out the gift of the Holy Ghost. For they heard them speak with tongues, and magnify God... (Acts 10:44-46).

And as I began to speak, the Holy Ghost fell on them, as on us at the beginning (Acts 11:15).

He [Paul] *said unto them, Have ye received the Holy Ghost since ye believed? And they said to him, We have not so much as heard whether there be any Holy Ghost. And he said unto them, Unto what then were ye baptized? And they said, Unto John's baptism. Then Paul said, John verily baptized with the baptism of repentance, saying unto the people, that they should believe on Him which should come after him, that is, on Christ Jesus. When they heard this, they were baptized in the name of the Lord Jesus. And when Paul had laid his hands upon them, the Holy Ghost came on them; and they spoke with tongues, and prophesied* (Acts 19:2-6).

Through mighty signs and wonders, by the power of the spirit of God; so that from Jerusalem, and round about unto Illyricum, I have fully preached the gospel of Christ (Romans 15:19).

And my speech and my preaching was not with enticing words of man's wisdom, but in demonstration of the Spirit, and of power: that your faith should not stand in the wisdom of men, but in the power of God (1 Corinthians 2:4-5).

For the kingdom of God is not in word, but in power (1 Corinthians 4:20).

This only would I learn of you, received ye the Spirit by the works of the law, or by the hearing of faith? (Galatians 3:2)

God hath sent forth the Spirit of His Son into your hearts, crying Abba, Father (Galatians 4:6).

But as then he that was born after the flesh persecuted him that was born after the Spirit, even so it is now (Galatians 4:29).

Stand fast therefore in the liberty wherewith Christ hath made us free, and be not entangled again with the yoke of bondage (Galatians 5:1).

...Walk in the Spirit, and ye shall not fulfil the lust of the flesh (Galatians 5:16).

Now unto Him that is able to do exceeding abundantly above all that we ask or think, according to the power that worketh in us, unto Him be glory in the church by Christ Jesus throughout all ages, world without end (Ephesians 3:20-21).

...Grieve not the Holy Spirit of God... (Ephesians 4:30).

For unto you it is given in the behalf of Christ, not only to believe on Him, but also to suffer for His sake (Philippians 1:29).

Be careful for nothing; but in every thing by prayer and supplication with thanksgiving let your requests be made known unto God (Philippians 4:6).

For in Him dwelleth all the fullness of the Godhead bodily (Colossians 2:9).

Take heed to the ministry which thou hast received in the Lord, that thou fulfil it (Colossians 4:17).

...Praying also for us, that God would open unto us a door of utterance, to speak the mystery of Christ, for which I am also in bonds (Colossians 4:3).

For our gospel came not unto you in word only, but also in power, and in the Holy Ghost, and in much assurance; as you know what manner of men we were among you for your sake (1 Thessalonians 1:5).

For this cause also thank we God without ceasing, because, when ye received the Word of God which ye heard of us, ye received it not as the word of men, but as it is in truth, the Word of God, which effectually worketh also in you that believe (1 Thessalonians 2:13).

In every thing give thanks: for this is the will of God in Christ Jesus concerning you (1 Thessalonians 5:18).

For God has not given us the spirit of fear; but of power, and of love, and of a sound mind (2 Timothy 1:7).

Yea, and all that will live Godly in Christ Jesus shall suffer persecution (2 Timothy 3:12).

Thou hast loved righteousness, and hated iniquity; therefore God, even thy God, hath anointed thee with the oil of gladness above thy fellows (Hebrews 1:9).

For unto us was the gospel preached, as well as unto them: but the word preached did not profit them, not being mixed with faith in them that heard it (Hebrews 4:2).

But without faith it is impossible to please Him; for he that cometh to God must believe that He is, and that He is a rewarder of them that diligently seek Him (Hebrews 11:6).

1. "God, I believe that You exist!"

2. "God, I believe that You are a rewarder of those who diligently seek You!"

Jesus Christ the same yesterday, and to day, and for ever (Hebrews 13:8).

The glory of this latter house shall be greater than of the former, saith the Lord of hosts: and in this place will I give peace, saith the Lord of hosts (Haggai 2:9).

...the yoke shall be destroyed because of the anointing (Isaiah 10:27).

But the anointing which ye have received of Him abideth in you, and ye need not that any man teach you: but as the same anointing teacheth you of all things, and is truth, and is no lie, and even as it hath taught you, ye shall abide in Him (1 John 2:27).

...This is the word of the Lord...Not by might, nor by power, but by my spirit, saith the Lord of hosts (Zechariah 4:6).

And I will raise Me up a faithful priest [A Young Warrior], **that shall do according to that which is in Mine heart and in My mind:** *and I will build him a sure house; and he shall walk before mine anointed forever* (1 Samuel 2:35).

Appendix A

A Brief Statement of Faith Presbyterian Church (U.S.A.) (1983)

"In life and in death we belong to God.
    Through the grace of our Lord Jesus Christ,
        the love of God,
            and the communion of the Holy Spirit,
    we trust in the one triune God, the Holy One of Israel,
        whom alone we worship and serve.

"We trust in Jesus Christ,
    fully human, fully God.
Jesus proclaimed the reign of God;
    preaching good news to the poor
        and release to the captives,
    teaching by word and deed
        and blessing the children,
    healing the sick
        and binding up the brokenhearted,

eating with outcasts
forgiving sinners,
and calling all to repent and believe the gospel.
Unjustly condemned for blasphemy and sedition,
Jesus was crucified,
suffering the depths of human pain
and giving His life for the sins of the world.
God raised this Jesus from the dead,
vindicating His sinless life,
breaking the power of sin and evil,
delivering us from death to life eternal.

"We trust in God,
whom Jesus called Abba, Father.
In sovereign love God created the world good
and makes everyone equally in God's image,
male and female, of every race and people,
to live as one community.
But we rebel against God; we hide from our Creator.
Ignoring God's commandments,
we violate the image of God in others and ourselves,
accept lies as truth,
exploit neighbor and nature,
and threaten death to the planet entrusted to our care.
We deserve God's condemnation.
Yet God acts with justice and mercy to redeem creation.
In everlasting love,
the God of Abraham and Sarah chose a covenant
people to bless all families of the earth.
Hearing their cry,
God delivered the children of Israel
from the house of bondage.

Loving us still,
>God makes us heirs with Christ of the covenant.
>Like a mother who will not forsake her nursing child,
>like a father who runs to welcome the prodigal home,
>>God is faithful still.

"We trust in God the Holy Spirit,
>everywhere the giver and renewer of life.
>The Spirit justifies us by grace through faith,
>>sets us free to accept ourselves and to love God and
>>>neighbor,
>>and binds us together with all believers
>>in the one body of Christ, the Church.
>The same Spirit
>>who inspired the prophets and apostles
>>rules our faith and life in Christ through Scripture,
>>engages us through the word proclaimed,
>>claims us in the waters of baptism,
>>feeds us with the bread of life and the cup of salvation,
>>and calls women and men to all ministries of the Church.
>In a broken and fearful world
>the Spirit gives us courage
>>to pray without ceasing,
>>to witness among all peoples to Christ as Lord and Savior,
>>to unmask idolatries in Church and culture,
>>to hear the voices of peoples long silenced,
>>and to work with others for justice, freedom, and peace.
>In gratitude to God, empowered by the Spirit,
>>we strive to serve Christ in our daily tasks
>>>and to live holy and joyful lives,
>>even as we watch for God's new heaven and new earth,
>>>praying, "Come, Lord Jesus!"

"With believers in every time and place,
   we rejoice that nothing in life or in death
   can separate us from the love of God in Christ Jesus our Lord.

Glory be to the Father, and to the Son, and to the Holy Spirit.
   Amen"*

*Instead of saying this line, congregations may wish to sing a version of the Gloria.

Appendix B

The Nicene and the Apostles' Creeds

The Nicene Creed
(A.D. 381)

"We believe in one God the Father Almighty, Maker of heaven and earth, and of all things visible and invisible; And in one Lord Jesus Christ, the only-begotten Son of God, begotten of the Father before all worlds, God of God, Light of Light, Very God of Very God, begotten, not made, being of one substance with the Father, by whom all things were made; who for us men, and for our salvation, came down from heaven, and was incarnate by the Holy Spirit of the Virgin Mary, and was made man, and was crucified also for us under Pontius Pilate. He suffered and was buried, and the third day He rose again according to the Scriptures, and ascended into heaven, and sitteth on the right hand of the Father. And He shall come again with glory to judge both the quick and the dead, whose kingdom shall have no end.

"And we believe in the Holy Spirit, the Lord and Giver of Life, who proceedeth from the Father and the Son, who with the Father and the Son together is worshipped and glorified, who spoke by the prophets. And we believe in one holy catholic and apostolic Church. We acknowledge one baptism for the remission of sins. And we look for the resurrection of the dead, and the life of the world to come. Amen."

The Apostles' Creed
(Around A.D. 180, Revised in 8th Century)

"I Believe in God the Father Almighty, Maker of heaven and earth, And in Jesus Christ his only Son our Lord; who was conceived by the Holy Ghost, born of the virgin Mary, suffered under Pontius Pilate, was crucified, dead, and buried; He descended into hell; the third day He rose again from the dead; He ascended into heaven, and sitteth on the right hand of God the Father Almighty; from thence He shall come to judge the quick and the dead. I believe in the Holy Ghost; the holy catholic Church; the communion of saints; the forgiveness of sins; the resurrection of the body; and the life everlasting. Amen."

Appendix C

Facts About Biblical Anointing

*I*n the Old Testament the anointing was performed by a prophet or a priest who poured oil over the top of the candidate's head. This was a special oil of the highest quality, the finest grade of purity. It was mixed with myrrh and other expensive spices and was used exclusively by the priests in their anointing ceremonies. The great value of the oil signified the importance that the Lord placed upon the person receiving it.

(The actual ingredients are myrrh, cinnamon, calamus, cassia, and olive oil. Actual recipe: 250 ounces of myrrh, 125 ounces of cinnamon, 125 ounces of calamus, 250 ounces of cassia, and 6 quarts of olive oil.)

The Holy Spirit then descended upon the person and from that day forward he was anointed to serve.

Psalm133 describes this ceremony in a vivid and poetic way:

> *...Behold, how good and how pleasant it is for brethren to dwell together in unity! It is like the precious ointment upon the head, that ran down upon the beard, even Aaron's beard: that went down to the skirts of his garments; as the dew of Hermon, and as the dew that descended upon the mountains of Zion: for there the Lord commanded the blessing, even life for evermore.*

Christ literally means "anointed." The Greek word *Christos* comes from another root word, *Chrio*, which denotes the idea of contact—to smear or rub with oil— to consecrate to an office.

Chrio comes from the root word, *Chraomai*, meaning "to furnish what is needed—to light upon." And, finally, *Chraomai* comes from the root word, *phrisso*, which means "to bristle, or chill, shudder, or tremble."

Putting all of this together, we can easily understand that when a person is anointed, he is contacted by the living God from outer space who "smears or rubs" him with oil and consecrates him for service. This God has furnished him with what is needed to perform any task that He asks him to perform because He (God the Holy Spirit) has come upon him. Receiving a touch of the supernatural power of God is awesome and every person reacts differently. But the *phrisso* implies a physical as well as a spiritual and emotional feeling. Why should we be surprised if the one receiving the anointing bristles, chills, shudders, or trembles? I certainly have no problem with it.

Actually, we should be surprised if a person does not "tremble" while he is being anointed. Who can remain unmoved upon receiving a personal touch from the hand of the living God of the universe?

When crowning a new king, the anointing with oil was the religious act and always came first. It preceded the coronation ceremony, which was the political act. The political ceremony acknowledged what God had already approved of. So often today it is done backwards. Someone is put into office, and then it is hoped that he will be used by the Lord. Later, when everyone is disappointed with the person's lack of achievement, they wonder what went wrong. It is somewhat like buttoning your shirt. If you start with the wrong buttonhole, it ends up uneven—although your intentions were good.

Destiny Image
Revival Books

WHEN THE HEAVENS ARE BRASS

by John Kilpatrick.

Pastor John Kilpatrick wanted something more. He began to pray, but it seemed like the heavens were brass. The lessons he learned over the years helped birth a mighty revival in Brownsville Assembly of God that is sweeping through this nation and the world. The dynamic truths in this book could birth life-changing revival in your own life and ministry!

Paperback Book, 168p. ISBN 1-56043-190-3 (6" X 9") Retail $9.99

WHITE CANE RELIGION
And Other Messages From the Brownsville Revival

by Stephen Hill.

In less than two years, Evangelist Stephen Hill has won nearly 100,000 to Christ while preaching repentance, forgiveness, and the power of the blood in what has been called "The Brownsville Revival" in Pensacola, Florida. Experience the anointing of the best of this evangelist's life-changing revival messages in this dynamic book!

Paperback Book, 182p. ISBN 1-56043-186-5 Retail $8.99

PORTAL IN PENSACOLA

by Renee DeLoriea.

What is happening in Pensacola, Florida? Why are people from all over the world streaming to one church in this city? The answer is simple: *Revival!* For more than a year, Renee DeLoriea has lived in the midst of the revival at Brownsville Assembly of God. *Portal in Pensacola* is her firsthand account of this powerful move of the Spirit that is illuminating and transforming the lives of thousands!

Paperback Book, 182p. ISBN 1-56043-189-X Retail $8.99

Available at your local Christian bookstore.

Internet: http://www.reapernet.com

Prices subject to change without notice.

Destiny Image
New Releases

THE CROSS IS STILL MIGHTIER THAN THE SWITCHBLADE
by Don Wilkerson.
Don Wilkerson, co-director of the original Brooklyn Teen Challenge with his brother David, tells of the ministry's incredible growth and success in working with troubled youth today. With current eyewitness reports and testimonies of former addicts and gang members, he proves that *The Cross Is Still Mightier Than the Switchblade.*
Paperback Book, 196p. ISBN 1-56043-264-0 Retail $8.99

THE GUNS OF GOD!
by George Otis.
Learn how to wage spiritual warfare against the attacks of the evil one! Too many people are shackled in sin and bound by addictions; Christians need to rise up in the power of God and proclaim victory! Clearly and concisely, George Otis cuts through today's confusing theories about spiritual warfare and explains how to do it!
Paperback Book, 144p. ISBN 1-56043-281-0 Retail $7.99

SHARE THE FIRE
by Guy Chevreau.
Do you panic when you hear the word *evangelism*? Do you feel awkward "forcing" your opinions on another? All that changes when God abundantly and freely fills you with His Spirit! In *Share the Fire* you'll learn how God has intended evangelism to be: a bold and free work of Christ in you and through you!
Paperback Book, 182p. ISBN 1-56043-688-3 Retail $8.99

THE FINAL VICTORY: THE YEAR 2000
by Marvin Byers.
Can we know the time of Christ's coming as John the Baptist, Simeon, Anna, and others knew? Jesus is standing at the door. But who knows the time of His return? Will we make the same mistakes as those who missed Him the first time? Find the answers in this revolutionary study of the last days.
Paperback Book, 336p. ISBN 1-56043-824-X (6" X 9") Retail $14.99

Available at your local Christian bookstore.
Internet: http://www.reapernet.com
Prices subject to change without notice.

A short-term mission trip is one of the very best things that you can do with your life. We have taken over 1,000 people to China, and we have spearheaded mission teams to 45 other nations.

If you write or call, we will give you all of the details. You may soon find yourself traveling with a team of Young Warriors to a very exciting place in the world.

You can go!

Wesley Smith
Full Life Crusade
P.O.Box 398
Winona Lake, Indiana 46590
Tel. 219-267-7546, 518-696-4973
E-mail: Wes@KConline.com